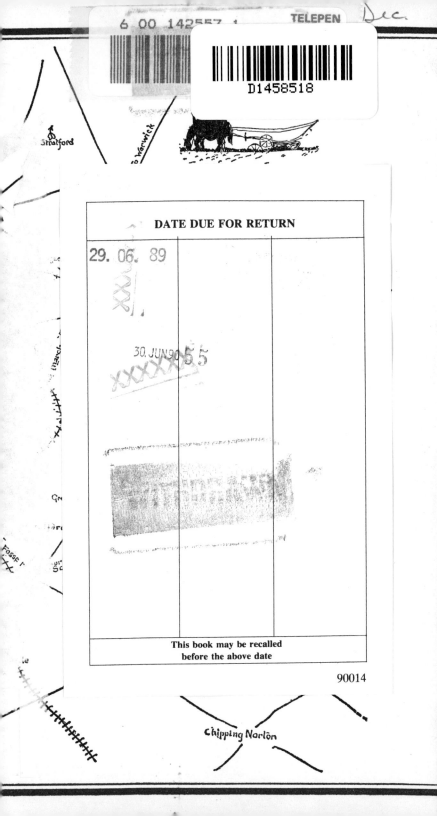

Stratford

Warwick

DATE DUE FOR RETURN

This book may be recalled
before the above date

Fosse

Chipping Norton

A Square Mile of Old England

A Square Mile of Old England

... less four acres

Aubrey Seymour

illustrated by himself

edited by Margaret Baker

Kineton : The Roundwood Press

1972

Aubrey Seymour also wrote:

THE LAND WHERE I BELONG, 1968

FRAGRANT THE FERTILE EARTH, 1970

SBN 900093 39 0

Set in 'Monotype' Bembo, series 270, and printed by
Gordon Norwood at The Roundwood Press, Kineton, in the County of Warwick
and bound by Eric Neal at Welford

Made and printed in England

Contents

INTRODUCTION

The Child is father of the Man
WORDSWORTH

WE LIVED IN THE COUNTRY on the outskirts of Leamington when I
was a small boy. Our house was on one side of the road and my
father's three grass fields on the other, but I was not allowed to
cross over to them to play until the spring was well advanced. Then
there would come a balmy morning and to my intense delight the
ban would be lifted. My first act always was to throw myself on
my tummy, bury my nose in the young clover and grass and smell.
How delicate was the scent of plant life bursting from the earth!
I would lie there inhaling till a voice called, "Get up from that damp
grass, you naughty boy!" I suppose it would be in April that my
release came, because I remember once that the first swallow was
quartering the field about six inches above the ground and I
noticed how its blue back contrasted with the short, dark-green
grass, and of course the sky was full of larks.

When I was a little older, the primitive urge to hunt came upon
me and I toiled up to the boundary fence and bought a large, hazel
bean-stick for a penny from the old market-gardener on the other
side; with that and a piece of strong string I made me a powerful
bow. Arrows presented no problem, as we had a quiverful of
Indian ones which my father had brought back from the Rocky
Mountains, fearful-looking things with barbs of an inch or more

and reputed to be poisoned; there was another quiver of archery arrows, a little longer in the shaft and with normal heads. Whether or not the Indian specimens were really poisoned, we never established; certainly we never came to any harm from them. My brothers also had bows and, so equipped, we were ready for anything; imagination converted the three fields into prairies stocked with buffaloes and braves and we became, in our own eyes at least, mighty hunters.

Other boys sometimes joined us. A certain mother's darling wore a straw hat and one day when I saw it advancing towards me through the long grass I took a shot at it. My aim was better than usual. The hat was tipped back on the wearer's head and the arrow passed through the brim and into the crown, the point came out in the middle and there stuck. When the victim of my prowess got home, his fond mother wanted to know what had happened and it was some weeks before he was allowed to play with those rough young Seymours again.

One of my favourite games was to stalk the rooks and take long shots at them, but they always seemed to see the approaching missiles. I got a lot of exercise retrieving my arrows.

Occasionally we varied our hunting by shooting vertically into the sky to see how near us the arrow would fall; an allowance had to be made for the wind. Once my brother Donald was too successful, for as he was gazing up at the falling arrows he called out that he had lost sight of his and the next moment it landed on the inside of his cheek-bone and went under his eye. How the blood gushed out! Fortunately the eye was not damaged, but he bore a scar all his life, as prominent as the one left by a German bullet many years after. Our practice taught us a lot about elevation and alignment, which was useful when we advanced to guns.

I well remember the first time, while still only a small boy, that I went on a real hunting expedition; it was on a Whit Monday and the members of a syndicate took me with them on their rough shoot. There was no keeper on it, so they used to go over from time to time and kill what vermin they could themselves. On this occasion they were after magpies and crows and also hoped to get a few young rabbits.

One member, a canny Scot, who was fond of a joke, suggested a sweepstake, the proceeds to go to the one who shot the heaviest rabbit. The shoot was divided into several beats, lots were drawn for them, and at the end of the day a row of miserable little corpses was laid out. The Scotsman claimed to have the heaviest, although there were several obviously larger ones and, as nothing else would satisfy him, some balances were borrowed. When his pot-bellied specimen pulled up one of the larger ones with a bump, the rest of the party became suspicious and insisted on examining it; they found it had been paunched and neatly stitched up again after several stones had been put in!

I expect it was all for my benefit!

Though my father was in business, he was a countryman at heart and the three fields where we played were run as a hobby farm. Among other livestock, he kept a house cow, poultry and a styful of pigs. It was my job to feed the hens and collect the eggs. All the Old English game birds belonged to me and it was my delight to see my game cock heading his harem home; no hen dared to walk in front of him. He lifted each foot with deliberation, careful not to hit one spur against the other, and when he found a tit-bit he would call up a favourite hen and, after much chortling, give it to her. He was a magnificent bird with his golden hackles and black breast.

A walk we often took was through Tachbrook village and along the lane that led to Oakley Wood, passing some half-dozen cottages, each standing in its own bit of ground at intervals of several hundred yards. In every back-garden there were a few hens of no recognisible breed, presided over by a cock of doubtful lineage, and every cottager seemed to rear one brood a year to replace the birds that had been eaten—it was part of the rural economy. I got to know each cock and tried to work out its ancestry. One obviously had a big streak of Indian Game in him and he passed it on to his progeny, which were square-shouldered and proud breasted; another, with his heavily-barred plumage, showed a good deal of Plymouth Rock, a breed very popular at the time. My father had a pen of them and I can visualise their big, brown eggs even now, but, if I remember rightly, the hens did not lay enough of them, being inclined to stop at a dozen or so and then go broody. I parted with some of my pocket-money every week for a copy of 'The Feathered World'; I liked particularly the illustrations of Silver-spangled Hamburgs. It is understandable that I was not very impressed with the cottagers' mongrels.

In the corner of one of my father's fields, up by the allotments there was a water-trough supplied by a pump and my father gave me sixpence a week to keep the trough full. The job was really beyond my strength and it was exasperating on a really hot day to watch the big bullocks drinking as fast as I could pump. Another thing that vexed me was that after I had filled the trough a hulking man would appear from the allotments with two big buckets; he did not use the pump, oh, no! he filled them from the water I had so laboriously drawn, and although it was back in the 1890's, the sense of annoyance is as sharp as if it had happened yesterday.

The pumping had its compensations, for the adjacent hedge was the nesting place of hedge-sparrows, chaffinches, bullfinches and linnets. White-throats and yellow-hammers nested in the ditch on the far side and lecherous sparrows in the barn.

It was all a very long time ago and the huge Lockheed works now covers the fragrant earth of my old stamping ground, where I took my first lessons in becoming a countryman.

CHAPTER ONE

I take Possession

MY BROTHERS AND I attended Warwick School, but it was so evident that a classical education was a waste of my father's money and my time that I left at fifteen to become a farm pupil. I spent a year near Leicester and another in Manitoba, and at eighteen, with my father's backing, I launched out as a tenant farmer at Westfields, near Kineton. Two years here gave me much valuable experience, and having proved that I was right in choosing farming as my career, my father decided to buy me a place of my own.

Farming was only 'change for a shilling' at the time and it was easier to lose money than to make it; if it had not been a way of life, the countryside might have become derelict. There were plenty of properties on the market and my father and I spent a lot of time cycling here and there to view such as seemed suitable from the estate agent's description, but we did not find what we wanted. Then one morning an elaborate, illustrated catalogue arrived, advertising the sale of half a dozen farms on the south-western boundary of Warwickshire; they belonged to a Mr Hayden Best, an elderly man, who wanted to realise his holdings for the benefit of his nephews and nieces.

My father and I got on our cycles again and a long, rough ride we had of it. We set off from Bromson Hill along the old Fosse Way, a bad road at that time with gates across it; grass grew on either side of the clear strip where the horse travelled and there were two accompanying tracks, worn by the wheels of vehicles. We patiently wobbled along some eighteen miles till we came to Ditchford-on-Fosse. The farm here was not suitable, so we turned off the Fosse on to an even less-used road, known as Galloping Lane, which ran along the crest of a ridge. This took us to Little

The Old Fosse Way, 1908.

Ditchford and beyond till we looked down on Upper Ditchford Farm. There was no obvious road to it, but going by the map, we picked up a very bumpy track across two fields and so dropped down to the buildings.

We found Mr Barratt, the old farmer, at home and very glad to see us. He wanted to get out of his lease, which still had seven years to run, and when he saw we were interested he offered to let us in at Lady Day, although he was a Michaelmas tenant, provided we would take all his live and dead stock. He conducted us over the farm and his introductory remark as we passed through every gate was 'Now this is a reaming good field!' Before we turned for home the bargain was made. His stock was well-bred and his implements in working order, if somewhat old-fashioned, and we agreed that the Shipston auctioneer, Frank Parsons, should act for us both, a proof of the esteem in which he was held.

I do not know the derivation of 'reaming', but it was clear that in describing the fields as 'reaming good' Mr Barratt meant us to understand that they were something out of the ordinary. There is another odd word that I have heard used locally as a superlative. I had been after some pigeons one day and owing to scarcity of cover I had had to shoot at the birds as they whirled over a high hedge with the wind behind them. An old chap hanging a gate greeted me as I was returning home.

'I 'eard you cracking away to 'em,' he said, then appraising my bag, he added, 'you ain't done so bad.'

'I should have done better if they'd been flying into the wind,' I replied.

'Aye,' he agreed; 'they be birds that can fly most i-zable fast sometimes!'

I lived with the farmer and his wife for a fortnight before the official date for moving in, so that I could get a little used to the place, and I still remember their wonderful, sugar-cured hams, two or three years old. I found a few snags, of course, that Mr Barratt had not mentioned as he was enthusing about his fields, for instance, that there was no proper road to the place; when my father and I cycled there we had come down to the farm from the back and had taken it for granted that there was a better approach at the foot of the hill. All the same I was well satisfied, it was a good farm and had some of the best land in the district.

The course of the stream, the Neighbrook, (Kneebrook on the Ordnance map) running roughly west to east along the valley bottom, marked the southern boundary of the property, except for one small field. I say advisedly that the brook ran roughly east to west for it made so many detours that its length must have been at least twice the distance it covered, measured 'as the crow flies.' Galloping Lane on its ridge also ran west and east, cutting my land in two; my northern limit was the Paddle Brook.

The house was a rambling old place that had been added to from time to time; it was stone-built with a red roof that had evidently replaced one of Stonefield tiles. It is a great pity to see these old roofs go, but the cost of repairing is prohibitive, as the timber carrying the great weight of the stones may need renewal and old tiles for replacement are very hard to come by.

An ancient wisteria climbed over one side of the house and up the porch. At the back was an enormous, mullioned window that reached from the ground to the roof and served both the cellar and the staircase; the lead lights were all of old, green-tinted glass. The cellar steps were saucer-shaped in the centre, worn away by the number of barrels of cyder that had been let down them; when I took over, all I found was a lot of newts on the damp floor.

The kitchen, unlike those of many old farm-houses, was poor and not the room originally used as such; that had been served by the present front-door, with another door opposite into a back kitchen and so to an exit into the yard. The alterations we made still left a run-through, fortunately as it turned out, for a heavy April snow-storm, followed by a sudden thaw, brought a torrent of water against the back of the house and we were able to prevent the whole of the ground floor being swamped by opening the front-door and allowing the water to escape. I had no mind to let such a crisis arise again and cut a ditch to direct future floods into the pond instead of into the house.

Some of the rooms had been used as granaries by my predecessor, William Timms; he also had several years' wool clip stored in one of the bedrooms. The wool was bought eventually by a Mr Bomford, who told me that when he came to take it away, he stood down below, packing it in big sheets, while Timms threw the, fleeces out of the window—till he got tired, then he shouted down 'There, that's the lot!' though several sheets of wool were left! The fact was that Timms did not need the money, so what was the use of going to the trouble of getting more? Does this illustrate the philosophy of those who farm for the love of the life?

The less said about many of the farm buildings the better. There were two groups, one at the back of the house and the other on the far side of Galloping Lane. Those behind the house consisted of cow-sheds for thirty animals, half-a-dozen pig-sties and an open yard, all very primitive as the farm was mostly grass. The buildings over the hill were quite another matter; there was an open shed, a yard with a water-trough in one corner, and a good brick barn with sliding doors, each with a smaller door inset that enabled one to pass in and out without too much disturbance when the wind was in a frolic.

And so, at the age of twenty, I found myself the owner of a 'reaming good' farm of two hundred and fifty-six acres, most of the fields facing south, and a mile of trout stream thrown in for full measure. I had two experienced, elderly men to help me, Thomas Beasley, whom I had 'taken over' with the stock, and 'old Beale' from Draycott, two miles away. One thing I did not take over with the place was its name. There were far too many Ditchfords in the area, Middle Ditchford, Ditchford Hill, Ditchford-on-Fosse, Ditchford Mill, and I soon found my mail for Upper Ditchford going astray. I changed from a ditch to a stream and called my new home Neighbrook.

CHAPTER TWO

This little pig stayed at home
NURSERY RHYME

MY FATHER MUST HAVE been finding it an expensive matter to start
four sons out in the world. At the same time that he was providing
money to set me up in farming, my eldest brother, Wallace, the
only academic member of the family, was studying at St. Andrew's
University and my younger brothers were hankering for a
planter's life in the West Indies.

Temporarily Leonard and Donald threw in their lot with me.
My mother found a housekeeper for us, but her choice was un-
fortunate as she had taken pity on a poor old wreck, who had not
the foggiest notion how to cater for three hungry men. The climax
came when she produced two enormous roly-poly puddings one
day. As she put them on the table, lying side by side on a dish,
Donald said, 'Twins!' and the old girl burst into tears and rushed
from the room; she left next day, I think she had been engaged as
unlikely to lead any of us astray, but in her next choice my mother
went to the other extreme and picked a very attractive young
woman, as good-looking as she was capable. She left hurriedly,
too. Mother came to stay with us and they must have had words,
for when I came in to tea, the good-looker had gone!

This second domestic crisis happened just as Leonard and
Donald were about to leave me for St. Lucia and their going

6

opened the way to an arrangement with a better prospect of permanence. We decided—for I had begun to have a say in things—that the house could easily be divided, and a man and wife and teenage son moved into one part, while I occupied the other. The woman was a good cook and her husband a capable cowman, while the son worked as a farm hand.

I did not envy my brothers some of their early experiences. Their first night at St. Lucia was hardly restful. They had candles to light them to bed and great fat moths, with bodies like small cigars, tried to commit suicide by flying into them and putting them out. Finally Leonard decided to settle down in darkness and was no sooner asleep than something, very much alive and weighing not far short of a pound, dropped from the ceiling on to his chest. He hastily re-lit the candle and found a handsome green lizard that had come in search of some of the disabled moths; it could not climb up on to the bed, as the legs were standing in jars of disinfectant to keep away the bugs, a common pest in the islands, so it had walked up the wall and along the ceiling and dropped down from there.

These lizards are big enough to frighten anyone meeting them for the first time, but they are quite harmless; not so the small West Indian snakes which live in the vegetation at the sides of the clearing and are apt to strike with deadly consequence at anything that disturbs them. They are not native, but were introduced earlier to keep the slaves from running off into the jungle.

Wallace, too, was soon abroad, for he passed the Indian Civil Service examinations and was posted to Ceylon where he, too, learnt at first-hand about tropical fauna. His most alarming experience was when he walked, stark naked, into his bathroom and met a tarantula. He told me he never felt so helpless in his life until he fetched a golf-club and managed to dispatch the intruder. Its hairy body filled a large teacup! Another unwelcome squatter was a cobra which took up residence in one of the drain-pipes close to his backdoor; but a pretty little green frog with vacuum toes, that

7

lived behind one of the pictures, made itself useful by darting out and seizing flies from the wall.

It is not altogether surprising that my brothers should choose to go so far from home; there was pioneer blood in their veins that would not be gainsaid. All my uncles had been globe-trotters, three had fought through the American War of Independence, and my father and mother had crossed the Atlantic a good many times before we grew up, as my father was interested in a gold mine in Colorado, which was all roses till water got in; after that it cost more to get rid of the water than the value of the gold that came out! One summer I was the only member of the family left in the Old Country. Like the little pig in the rhyme, I stayed at home, Warwickshire born, Warwickshire bred, as firmly rooted in Warwickshire soil as any of its hedgerow elms.

I grew more and more in love with Neighbrook as time went on, but the life was lonely after my brothers left me and, more for the sake of having someone with whom to natter than for anything else, I took a farm pupil, one Frank Gill. He was a charming companion, interested in every side of country life and, what is more, played a good game of chess; but there was a fly in the ointment—he was a drunkard. His family sent him a ten-pound cheque every month, which I cashed for him, and he usually went off to Moreton and got rid of most of it. He was very penitent afterwards and if he had a pound left he went across to Aston Magna and made sure it did not go the way of the rest by giving it to the Vicar for the Organ Fund. Then he would settle down till the next instalment.

He was a keen angler, and under his tuition I learnt the gentle art of fly-fishing. Though he caught quite a few trout in the brook, I cannot remember that he took anything really big, but he was a diligent trier and forgot what alcohol was like when so engaged.

When it came to guns, I could more than hold my own, for he was an indifferent shot. I am afraid we spent more time in sport than hard-working young farmers should and we went so far as to rent some rough shooting nearby. My father came over for a day with us and in the course of our outing he annoyed my companion by exclaiming sharply, 'Mind where you're pointing that gun!' The warning must have rankled, for two or three days later Frank tried to restore his self-esteem by accusing me of carelessness as we walked along side by side.

'Do you realise that if your gun went off now it would blow my head off?' he asked.

Without altering the angle of my gun, I pulled the trigger and the charge went harmlessly into the top of a willow-tree. Of course it was a foolish thing to do and he was so startled that I was afraid he was going to throw a fit, but I think it made him realise that he still had something to learn about fire-arms.

Frank was of an enquiring turn of mind and for some while his interest centred on hedgehogs. Gypsies are said to roll them in clay and bake them in red-hot ashes, and he went to the trouble of preparing an 'urchin' for the oven and asking my squeamish housekeeper to cook it for him. I am equally squeamish where food is concerned, but I tried a mouthful and should not have known it from rabbit. Though a full-grown hedgehog will weigh from one-and-a-half to two-and-a-half pounds, there is not much on them when the skin is removed.

Besides putting hedgehog on the menu—once—Frank established a live specimen in the dining-room, where it promptly got itself stuck behind an enormous Victorian sideboard. It could not back out because that would have rubbed up its prickles and we had to move the mahogany monstrosity to release the prisoner. When it became more at home in its new quarters, the hedgehog developed an amusing habit of creeping about under the carpet after black beetles. I was reminded of it years afterwards at a village fête where the competitors in an obstacle race had to worm their way beneath a huge wagon-sheet pegged down to the ground.

Except when domiciled in one's dining-room, or other confined space, it is difficult to keep hedgehogs under observation, as they do not wander abroad till after dusk; it is easier to track them down by ear than by eye since they snore when asleep and squeal and grunt when annoyed. They have few natural enemies. The fox gives them the go-by for obvious reasons, but I have heard they sometimes drop one in a pool of water so that it will uncurl to swim and can then be dispatched without injury to the attacker. Badgers, on the other hand, make short work of them, pulling them open with their powerful claws and forearms. I have often found the prickly skins turned inside out, a sure sign that a badger has been at work.

The carelessness and credulity of man are what the 'urchins' have most to fear and it is as well for the continuation of the species that they have litters of up to seven a year. In these latter times the motorcar takes a heavy toll, but the worst menace is the game-keeper, who, instead of being grateful to them for keeping down small vermin, accuses them on purely circumstantial evidence of stealing the eggs of ground-nesting birds. No doubt a hedgehog sometimes blunders on a sitting partridge and if an egg is broken in the flurry of the encounter, it is as acceptable to a hedgehog as to a rat, but, unlike the rat, the hedgehog had not hunted for the tit-bit. The farmer, also, is all too ready to jump to conclusions and maintains that hedgehogs suck the milk from recumbent cows. Hedgehogs do nothing of the sort! But should a hedgehog come upon a little milk oozed out on to the grass from the distended udder of a sleeping cow, it naturally clears up the mess. Gilbert White mentions such cases in his 'Natural History of Selborne.' A young veterinary surgeon of my acquaintance, who has to deal with many cows suffering from alleged hedgehog bites, declares that most such injuries have been inflicted by the cow's own hoof as she struggles to rise; and he has demonstrated that a hedgehog's mouth is too small to accommodate the teat and make a wound an inch or more from the tip, the usual place where it is found. But tradition dies hard, be the evidence what it may, and the poor 'urchin's bad, though unmerited, reputation still persists.

My enterprising farm pupil did not confine his interests to hedge-hogs, but brought indoors another much maligned creature, a snake. It was not long before it disappeared from its box in the dining-room and my housekeeper declared that she would not set foot there again till we found it. We never did, and it was four days before she plucked up courage to enter, in spite of our assurances that it was not an adder, but a grass snake and quite harmless, and that, in any case, it had managed to make good its escape.

CHAPTER THREE

There is no secret so close as between a rider and his horse

R. S. SURTEES

THOUGH THE STOCK I had taken over with Neighbrook was good, it was not what I really wanted and I soon sold most of it. I had no option with the cattle for they had contracted infectious abortion and fifteen had to go for slaughter straight away. I did not restock immediately, but rested the farm for the best part of a year by making a lot of hay. In the autumn, I bought a hundred good Masham theaves (first year ewes) from the north, ninety young Irish cattle, among them thirty good, dairy, shorthorn heifers, and, partly because it was such a nuisance to take my sows elsewhere, a Large White Boar. The only thing I brought with me from Westfields was a handsome, black, pedigree mare, registered and in foal.

With so much going out and as yet, so little coming in, I turned some of my timber to account and sold a number of hedgerow elms in Pond Ground, which lay immediately behind the house; they were getting past their best, but brought in a welcome three-hundred-and-fifty pounds. A big, burly, good-tempered fellow, called Bramble, came to haul away the butts, several of which contained three or four hundred feet of timber. He was the best man I ever knew with horses and I am afraid I wasted more than a few hours watching him work his team, if watching a display of sheer understanding and artistry could be called a waste of time.

His horses were always in splendid fettle and I was completely fascinated by the way they understood their job. Bramble would hitch six of them—two teams when they got out on to the hard road—to a large butt lying where it had been felled, sometimes in a ditch. What secret words of command he used I never could make out, but the horses knew what he meant and obeyed instantly. At one word the thiller, that is the one nearest the load, would lean into the collar, just enough to tighten the traces; at another word the next horse would do the same, and so on till the leader's traces were taut. Bramble would talk to them till every one of the six had got its legs well under it and, that done, he would let out such a yell as would have made John Peel green with envy and, if the traces did not burst, that tree had got to move! Once it had started in its way, with a crack of his whip and the sheer power of his drive, he would see to it that it was not allowed to come to rest till he had got it where he wanted it. Even if a trace did break, it only caused a short delay, for Bramble soon repaired it with a shut-link which he carried for just such an emergency.

When it came to rolling the huge butt up on to the timber-wagon, his complete command of the situation told again, for had the horses failed to stop dead the instant he called 'Whoa!' they would have pulled the wagon over on its side. Although quite firm with his team, I never knew him use his whip to thrash a horse and there was no plunging, nor wasted energy.

The last time I saw Bramble, he was driving an enormous steam tractor, a contraption that saved horse-power, but ruined drains and turf. It seemed a tragedy that such a superb horse-handler should have been compelled to sink to anything merely mechanical; I say 'compelled', as nothing will induce me to believe that he preferred the change. I knew of a Leamington drayman who, on drawing his wages on Saturday, always bought his horse a six-penny pork pie, which it ate with great relish. Sixpence made a hole in eighteen bob a week and it was an indication of the affection a good horseman can feel for his charge.

13

One of Bramble's sons went out to British Columbia. He recently contacted me and told me he is doing very well, fishing the Frazer River for salmon.

I was brought up in a horsey world, which is perhaps why I was able to derive so much pleasure from Bramble's masterly handling of his team. My father loved horses and always kept one or more, and my best friends at school, Sydney and Eddie MacGregor were sons of a race-horse breeder. I have a vivid memory of their stable-yard with a proud Old English game-cock scratching for bits for his favourite hen on the manure heap and a row of loose-boxes with a thoroughbred's head looking over every half-door. One horse was minus an eye, lost when it tried to savage its groom, who defended himself with a fork.

Eddie's father drove a four-in-hand, no mean feat of horseman-ship. He once drove his coach from Banbury to Leamington against a railway train, both setting off at the same time; of course every seat in the coach was booked in advance, but I cannot re-member if my father was one of the passengers. As they came down the steep slope from the canal bridge at Leamington and took the corner at the bottom, the near wheels were off the ground and everyone thought they were being tipped out, but all was well and they turned into the Crown Hotel yard as the train came thunder-ing over the bridges at the bottom of Bath Street.

The last time I saw old man MacGregor he was helping to get his daughter-in-law into an ambulance. She was winning the Ladies' Race at the Warwickshire Point-to-Point when her horse fell at the last fence. I never in my long life saw a man look so sad.

My father could not resist a horse deal and often bought in haste and found out the snags at leisure. There was, for instance, the time a young man rode up on a smart-looking four-year-old and persu-aded my father to put it in his dog-cart and go for a drive. My two brothers, at that time small children, went too—what my mother's reactions were afterwards, when she thought of what might have happened, I fail to imagine! Father was so pleased with the way the colt behaved that by the time they got back he had bought it. As it was being taken out of the shafts, the young man remarked, 'That's not bad for the first time in harness!'

I remember, years later, a young farmer asking my father to go and look at two three-year-old colts. He went and, although he could not detect any real faults, he thought them common brutes and decided not to buy them, but the farmer, probably in need of ready cash, implored him to make an offer. Eventually, just to choke the fellow off, my father bid exactly half the price asked. To his surprise the farmer jumped at it with, 'Hold your hand out!' Father was more suspicious than ever that he was being done, and his hand shot out and back again several times, like a snake's tongue, before he finally shook on the deal.

Things turned out better than could have been expected. We broke one of the colts into harness and sold it as a pitter for just what the two had cost; my father made me a present of the other, and after taking several nasty falls from it, I sold that one too, for the same amount.

Though I find my father's doubtful bargains amusing, I am not sure that I did any better myself. Looking back on the early days at Neighbrook, it seems that all our horses were too young, or too old. A piebald, a very fast horse, was involved in the first of several near-catastrophies in Little Ham, one of the fields below the house. Something upset it and it got off the road on to the turf; my brother Donald, who was in the trap, turned too sharply across a deep furrow to avoid going into the brook, and horse and trap went over on to their sides. The result was nothing worse than a broken shaft; but I did not get off so lightly the day my horse bolted as I was mounting. My right leg was badly wrenched and from time to time I have bouts of lameness, and now, at eighty-four, one leg is an inch and a half shorter than the other and I have a very stiff arthritic hip. It might have been a lot worse, for I get about with the aid of two thumb-sticks, and until quite recently, still drove my car.

CHAPTER FOUR

There was a jolly miller once . . .

ISAAC BICKERSTAFFE

NEIGHBROOK, AS WE HAD discovered as soon as we had bought it, had no proper access. A track of sorts led from the house to a bridge over the brook and across Joshua's Meadow, and brought one to within fifty yards or so of the Aston Magna–Paxford road. The intervening strip of land was part of Lord Redesdale's estate and it was only by courtesy that I crossed it. I approached his lordship's agent, John Kennedy, and through his good offices I was able to acquire enough ground to link my farm officially to the highway

I promptly set about improvements. Jack Bennett, the haulier from Paxford, spent a week or more bringing loads of broken, or misshapen bricks from the Aston Magna brickworks at one-and-six a load and I used to level them and make a few gouts to drain damp places on the upper side of the track to the turf on the other. It was a tedious job, but we finished up with eight-hundred yards of road that served our purpose very well, even if we could not call it a carriage drive.

The highway, when one got there, left much to be desired. The authorities 'mended' it, by putting down lumps of the local oolite stone, about the size of goose eggs, leaving them to be broken down by the traffic; no steam-roller ever came that way and if it had done so it would probably have got stuck. There was no keeping to the left; everything travelled down the middle and grass grew between the tracks made by the wheels and the horses hooves, as it did on the old Fosse Way. After frost, the oolite lifted and a peculiarly clinging mud resulted. I used to take a pride in my turn-out and started from home with clean wheels, but before I had got very far they were covered with the horrible muck, and my boots were in no better condition after I had opened a few gates. Adding the highway gates to those on my own property, there were nine to negotiate between the Neighbrook farmhouse and Aston Magna. If one was in a trap there were three operations to perform at each one; stop and open the gate, drive or lead the horse through, and then, trusting to Providence that the animal would not go on without you, go back and shut the gate. The procedure was so frustrating that, rather than catch a horse, saddle, or harness it and deal with those nine obstructions, I would often walk to Moreton-in-Marsh, or, for a longer journey, mount my cycle.

On a blustery March day, when I had chosen to provide my own horse-power, I was cycling along the main road near Mitford Bridge when the Reverend Mr Herrick, Vicar of Todenham, overtook me in his little (Wolseley) Stellite car. As he passed me, I thought, 'Dash it!' he's not going much faster than I am!' took firm grip of the handle-bars, put my head down—there was a very strong wind blowing in our faces—and trod hard on the pedals. I did not notice that he had pulled in and stopped and, before I knew where I was, I had ridden into him, shot over the folded hood and was inside his Reverence's car, cycle and all! He was livid! I think I can still hear his outraged, 'What are you doing in my car? You'll have to pay for this!'

I told him to take the car to the Crowhurst garage in Moreton-in-Marsh and get it repaired at my expense. I got off lightly on that score, as all the damage was a bent number-plate, but I and the cycle were another matter! I had a very sore chest where I had hit the folded hood of the car, and the upright part of the cycle frame had been bent back so that I could see the ball-bearings. Herrick had cooled down by the time he saw Crowhurst. 'Do you know a young fellow called Seymour?' he asked; 'and do you know any reason why he should try to commit suicide?'

Aston Magna and Paxford stood one at either end of that frustrating, gated, sticky-surfaced road that I had to travel every time I left my own fields, unless I struggled up to Galloping Lane, where conditions were different, but little better. We could see Aston Magna from Neighbrook, as it straggled across the slope of the hill on both sides of the railway line; Lord Redesdale had a brickyard there and when it was in full working there was always something going on in the village. Paxford, lying to the north of us, was nearer, but out of sight, and it had a blacksmith's forge and a shop that supplied an astonishnig variety of goods. There were several attractive houses and my old sporting mentor, P. J. B. Payne, lived in one with a Stonefield tile roof and mullioned windows, but no modern conveniences.

I remember being invited out there to supper one Sunday evening with a friend. The cooking arrangements were primitive and as we sat yarning before a roaring fire in the log-grate, Mrs P. J. appeared with an enormous saucepan containing the pudding and asked should we mind if she hung it on the hook over our fire. Of course we raised no objection; was not the pudding for our delectation? P. J.'s flow of good stories was unaffected by the interruption and he was in the middle of one of his sporting recollections, which went back to the days of flint-lock guns and pointer-dogs, when there was a muffled roar and the lid of the saucepan and the pudding went up the open and very sooty chimney! I can still see the bits of bright-yellow batter sticking to its blackened sides and hear P. J.'s comments, though I dare not record them! He was a master of invective; it was not so much what he said, as the way he said it. After one particularly violent outburst when we were out with a shooting party, an elderly acquaintance came up to me. 'I'm an old man,' he said—he was nearly ninety—'and I have heard some bad language in my time, but I have never heard anyone give such expression to it as your friend here!'

Needless to say, we never heard the end of P.J.'s story that evening, because after the explosion we all began to argue about the merits of baking-powder. I remember the supper was excellent —Porterhouse steak with onions, but, understandably, no pudding to follow. How many housewives nowadays know what a Porterhouse steak is? I remember that it had to have a little bit of sawn-off bone in one corner.

I passed only two buildings when going to or from Paxford. The one nearest the village was an old barn that had been converted into a cider factory by two men, Jim Slatter of Paxford and George Haines of Chipping Campden. They used fruit from the West Country where there were orchards each planted with a single variety of apple—Kingstone Black is the only one I remember. I have been told that a very special cider they produced was served to Oxford undergraduates as champagne.

But before reaching the old barn as I left home, I used to come to Bran Mill, which was served by the stream that came tumbling down Dovedale, above Blockley. In order to get the necessary fall of water, the buildings were set so far below the level of the road that one could look into the attic windows of the mill-house as one went by and my brothers and I often saw the miller's wife peering out as we rode, or drove, to Paxford; she told me many years afterwards that she had fallen in love with one of us! I expect it was my handsome brother Donald.

The buildings were old on a Saxon foundation, which would seem to show there had been a mill on the site for a very long while. It is claimed that it is one of the old woad mills. From my Prep. school days I remember that Julius Caesar came to Britain in 55 B.C. and reported that the inhabitants daubed themselves with blue woad; my dictionary provides the further details that woad is a cruciferous plant from which blue dye was produced until superceded by indigo fom the East; but where woad was grown and how it was processed I had no idea, nor, I think, has the average person. I am not so ignorant now. I learnt quite recently that it used to be cultivated in the Cotswolds and was a most profitable crop, realising up to £2 or more an acre, a lot of money a few hundred years ago. But there were snags. It could only be grown on the same ground for two years and had to be milled in remote places on account of the dreadful stink of the stuff while it was fermenting and drying. The siting of Bran Mill, near the suitable growing ground and far from habitation, fully supports the contention that it was once used for making the dye; further corroboration of the fact is that Dyer is a common name in the district. I have heard that there is a pub in Thame in Oxfordshire called 'The Blue Man;' could he be woaded?

Tom Randall, the miller, was as old-fashioned as his mill, rigged out in breeches and leggings and invariably white with flour. He was looked upon as a very knowledgeable sportsman and kept himself well informed by frequent visits to the jockey stables at Bourton-on-the-Hill, where a Mr Weaver trained several noted horses; indeed Tom was more interested in what was going to win the 3.30 than in attending to his gristing. He was blind in one eye, but the other was remarkably observant.

He hunted me up one morning. 'You're interested in birds,' he said. 'There's a pair of strange ones down by the fletcher pit; they're about the size of starlings, but with white breasts. They've been there a week or two and I reckon they must have a nest under the arch of the sluice-gate; you're bound to see them if you walk along there.'

I felt sure they must be dippers, or water-ousels, though I had never seen or heard of them in this part of the North Cotswolds, and I went off to the mill straight away. I was in luck, for there was a dipper excitedly bobbing about on the dead branch of an old, pollarded ash tree that overhung the water. I took it to be the cock and watched it for some time while it entertained me to a song, quite a sweet one; obviously it meant to let me know that this was his territory and I guessed there was a nest near, probably in the spray of the sluice-gate, over which a lot of water was falling. I

Dipper's nest.

Grey Wagtail's nest

soon spotted it, tucked away among the moss and lichen and roofed over to keep it dry. By holding on to a strong rail with one hand, I was able to reach down with the other and was just going to feel under the dome of the nest, when out tumbled four or five fully-fledged young dippers. They disappeared into the turmoil of water, only to come bobbing up like corks in the middle of the fletcher pit, where they were joined by both their agitated parents and enticed round the corner into the main stream and out of my sight.

The lonely situation of the one-time woad-mill had made its waters something of a nature reserve and I was always tempted to linger. The dippers nested near the sluice for a number of years after Tom Randall first came to tell me of them; that daintiest of British birds, the yellow wagtail, also made its home by the fletcher pit and the grey wagtail often broke its northward flight there in the spring. A well-trodden track from the pit to the mill-stream showed where the otters took a short cut overland. Tom tried to trap them several times but without success; sometimes the trap would be sprung, but beyond a few hairs there would be no sign of the otter—like the fox, it knew a thing or two! He had a stuffed specimen in a glass-case in his living-room, along with a white weasel and several birds, including a snow bunting. That particular otter had had no opportunity to use its intelligence to escape; Tom shot it while it was curled asleep in the top of a willow, its holt being under flood water.

Trout spawned in the shallows of the pit, their backs coming out of the water. I spent many hours watching them and I once glimpsed an enormous one, the largest I ever saw, leap the sluice. I used to fish there sometimes, but Tom was more adept, if less orthodox than I, and he knew just where and how to get a good trout when he wanted one. He told me he had taken them from below the big wheel itself when he had diverted the flow of water.

I caught a fish there once that rather puzzled me. It took a mayfly and put up a tremendous fight for its size—a little over half a pound —and was certainly a trout of some sort, though it was the colour of a dace. It had no markings of any description and was the same shade both belly and back, without the vestige of a spot. I gave it, with several others, to a friend, asking him to take special notice when he ate it; he told me later that it tasted like a very nice trout.

I remember one summer when there had not been rain for several weeks. The sun seemed to beat down hotter and hotter as time went on and the brook dwindled to a trickle. Tom could grind only for a short while each day and during the period the mill was in action, the fish below it were tempted to move about a bit; but they had to get back to their holes the moment the wheel stopped turning, or they were left stranded in the shallow pools on the edge of the stream.

A pair of carrion crows, themselves hard put to it to find a living, came punctually each morning and caught the stranded minnows. The big trout was also after the minnows, but only when the mill was working, and he was careful to get back to safety in good time. I tried for him more than once, but he was too wily for me, although he nearly made a mistake one day, following my minnow right up to my feet. Then he caught sight of me and was in such a hurry to turn that he splashed the water right up into my face. Other and better fishermen tried their luck with him, but he was never caught, unless the remains of a very large trout, left on the bank a little lower down the stream by an otter, was the last of him. If so, he must have been all of five pounds.

Some cases of specimen fish used to hang on the wall of a barber's shop in Banbury, and one day, when having my hair trimmed, I made a remark about this. Of course I had to hear the history of the hooking and landing of each one and when it came to the largest, a big trout from the Cherwell, I was given two versions of its capture. The owner of the estate on which it was caught and who had gone to the expense of having it mounted, had told a long tale of the fly he had used and the battle the fish had put up before being finally netted; but his gardener had a different story. 'He's a so-and-so liar,' he declared. 'I caught that trout after a flood. It was left stranded in a puddle and I pulled it out with a rake!'

Whichever tale one chose to believe, the fish was there, all the four or five pounds of it, to testify that it, at least, was no figment of the imagination, however much imagination had gone into the accounts of its demise.

Tom kept a few game fowl and probably supplied a change of blood now and then! There was still a little cock-fighting carried on behind the backs of the police and I know of several farms where there is an old cock-fighting pit to be seen. Tom also kept a Jersey cow—for more peaceful purposes—and Mrs Randall, as a great favour, let me have a pound of butter every week. I wish I could get some in these days, one could cut it half way, then break it and it would show the grain, or granules, as it should.

Tom lent me his gun on one occasion; it was an early Westley Richards and had a peculiar trigger pull-off; its motto should have been 'Wait for it!'

CHAPTER FIVE

Of Markets and Fairs

MY FARM PUPIL, Frank Gill, stayed with me for about a year and I much enjoyed his company. Then tragedy struck Neighbrook. My cowman developed galloping consumption and was dead in a week, the most distressing thing I ever saw. When Frank heard what was the matter, he bolted and I never heard from him again.

The cowman's wife and son no longer wished to stay with me and the loss of four members of my staff at a blow threw everything into chaos for a while, but after advertising I was able to engage an ex-army Irishman and his wife, as stockman and housekeeper respectively. The wife had been through a course in French cooking, which was not exactly the qualification I required, as I am conservative in the matter of food and find plain English fare all I need, but they settled down well enough, and with adequate help indoors and out, I found time to take my gun for a day's sport when I wanted. If pigeons or rabbits were the quarry, I could damp down qualms of conscience at my carefree way of life by persuading myself that thinning out such pests was really work.

Another frequent outing that could be excused on the grounds of necessity was attending market. I generally went to Moreton-in-Marsh, or Shipston-on-Stour, at both of which places the auctioneer was Frank Parsons, a John Bull if ever there was one. The market at Chipping Campden was also near, but at that time it was in the doldrums and reached such a state that the local farmers formed their own co-operative sales.

Moreton cattle market used to be held in the Main Street opposite the Redesdale Arms and a double row of trees, now demolished to make way for cars, provided a welcome shade in summer in which the animals were content to stand quietly for hours; but if the weather were hot and humid, a mischievous boy with a gift for imitation—and most villages had at least one—could cause instant pandemonium by buzzing like a gadfly. Then it was all tails straight up in the air and away for home by preference.

I have tried to pull off the trick myself, let me hasten to add, not on market day, but my efforts never caused the least alarm; maybe my buzzing was not as good as I thought, or perhaps I was not a judge of the required weather conditions. Even a perfect imitation will not fool cattle unless it is the kind of day to bring genuine gadflies into action.

I bought a number of good Irish cattle from time to time in Banbury market and if I did not buy in the ring, bought privately afterwards. I was always amused at the effrontery with which the Irishmen asked me ten pounds per head more than they were prepared to accept. They put the animals through the auction ring as a feeler, and, if they did not sell well, withdrew them, hoping to get better terms in a direct deal; but when trade was bad, they found themselves on a poor wicket, for if they were left with cattle on their hands, many of them had nowhere to send them them back to Ireland. A few of the biggest Irish dealers had their own farms in England, which made them independent and able to hold their animals for a more favourable market, or even have a good deal at the expense of their fellow countrymen.

Periodic Fairs supplemented the markets and drew dealers from a wide area and here Campden held its own with the annual Teg and Wool sales; the latter had survived from the far-off days when wool was wool and Chipping Campden the most important centre in the whole country. Moreton, Stow and Banbury had noted

Horse Fairs, the latter so often coinciding with the worst weather of the year that in a mild season the croakers would hold up a warning finger with, 'Wait till Banbury Fair!' In the 1880's the road crossing the high ground between Banbury and Shipston-on-Stour became blocked with drifted snow and a farmer, returning from the Fair, lost his life there. In those days people travelled in horse-drawn, open conveyances and it was no joke to be benighted in them.

A highlight of the Fairs was the Market Ordinaries, put on by the principal hotel proprietors, who vied with each other which could produce the best meal. Some important person always took the chair at the head of the table; he had to be a good carver, know all the diners and be able to keep the conversation going. At Moreton-in-Marsh, Mr Barlow was the one I remember most; he represented the Chipping Norton Brewery. One day when he did not turn up, the proprietress looked round to see whom else she should ask to carve two couple of ducks, accompanied by great tureens of green peas. I was in my early twenties and felt flattered when her choice fell on me, but devil a bit of duck did I get for myself! Before I had cut up the first, plates were coming back for second and third helpings. I verily believe some of the farmers had little business to transact, but a good gossip and a seat at the Market Ordinary was a pleasant change from the routine of work and a bit of relief to their wives.

No Moreton Fair was complete without a milk-float load of cheeses, brought in from Little Wolford by Mr Haines. Speaking from memory, the cost worked out at less than a shilling a pound, if one took a whole cheese, and the quality was excellent. There was an amusing tale of a group of farmers who stayed so late after one Fair day that they began to get hungry; a bit of bread and cheese was suggested, and when one of the celebrated Wolford products was brought in, a vast man from the Cotswolds helped himself so generously, urging the rest to follow suit, that some of the company could hardly smother their amusement. When the cheese was all but gone, the truth came out—it was his own cheese, fetched from his waiting trap, at which he had encouraged them to hack! He was not entertained!

Then there were the Fat Stock Shows. I recollect that John James of Whitchurch won First Prize with four shorthorns at Stratford, Shipston and Moreton, and repeated the performance with the same cattle the following year; they must have weighed nearly four ton!

In addition to markets, Fairs and Shows, occasional farm sales interrupted one's routine. There was one old chap, always at hand if he thought there was a chance of picking up a shilling or two, who was sure to be found at any sale held locally.

He would sometimes shove in a bid for a small lot and one day the auctioneer knocked down a pen of ducks to him, well knowing that he would never see the money for them. Nor did he, but curious to hear what the old fellow would say if tackled, he approached him some time later.

'When are you going to pay me for those ducks, Smith?' he asked.

'Oh, you must expect to make a bad debt now and then!' was the prompt reply.

On another occasion someone in a pub asked him if he ever by any chance paid for his beer himself.

'No,' answered Smith without a moment's hesitation, 'but I 'elps 'em get shut of it!'

*   *   *

Though I generally bought stock at market, I often found it paid to sell privately through a dealer, so saving the trouble and expense of transport and the auctioneer's commission; but I liked to attend market beforehand to get some idea of current prices.

Dealers have their specialities and one of the most important men, as far as cattle were concerned, was Frank Stroud of Banbury. Even when well over eighty years of age, he was still a regular attender at all the principal Midland markets; he once told me he moved, that is, bought and sold, as many as five hundred head of cattle in one week. If I had a good bunch of strong animals for sale, I used to send for Frank. He would stroll casually through them once, value them in his mind, ask me what I wanted for them, and then proceed to convince me that my swans were only geese. All the same I have sold him several thousand pounds' worth of cattle at one deal and I once had reason to regret not accepting his bid, for they brought considerably less money by auction a week later.

It was no use offering Frank anything but what we call in Warwickshire—good, strong, old cattle, bullocks for preference. He would dispose of them to the Northampton, or Leicester graziers, or sell them at his home, where he had an old turf hill at the back of the house that was an ideal place to show the animals to advantage to prospective purchasers. He liked to buy in the morning and sell in the evening—there were no flies on Frank!

He had several generations in the same way of business behind him. His great-grandfather was a noted horse dealer and is mentioned in the 'Annals of The Warwickshire Hunt.' He once sold six matched, black carriage horses to King Louis of France. He had scoured the country to find them—it is hard enough to match a single pair—and when he had them, he would not trust anyone but himself to deliver them. As they neared the French coast, a violent storm wrecked the boat, with great loss of life. Stroud managed to swim ashore, only to go through the siege of Paris in the stables prepared for the horses that had been drowned on their way to them.

Occasionally I sold a bunch of cattle to an old school-fellow of my father's, Sheldon Chapman of Thame, but they had to be outstandingly good. Unlike any of the other buyers with whom I dealt, I never had to say what I wanted for them; he would look them over and then tell me what he would give me, and I cannot recollect that he ever offered less than I had valued them myself. He had a very good farm where he could finish the beasts off and Thame market, only forty miles from London, was one of the best in England, regularly attended by butchers who liked to buy their beef on the hoof. I remember selling him several bunches of smart North Devons, which my father had sent me from Cullompton when he was living at Torquay, fine-looking red cattle with curly coats, small bone and light-coloured noses and horns.

When it was pigs I had ready for sale, Tom Andrews was my man. He was a good customer for all types; the fat ones went to Palethorpes to be converted into sausages. He was a great sportsman and had written a book on hunting, 'Gin and Beer,' the title being the name of a pack of hounds which he hunted round a bit of country so intersected by railways that Lord Coventry would not take the Croome pack there. Even so, he lent Tom hounds from time to time and I remember how upset the old boy was when one of them was killed on the line while in his care. Tough as he might be, he admitted, 'I daren't tell his Lordship!'

I had the tale from him when he came to my place to look over some store pigs, an errand that nearly ended in another disaster. The bargain struck, I had the job of putting the pigs on rail at Blockley. There were thirty or forty of them and we had no trouble in getting them to the station, but the pen from which we had to load them stood isolated on a bit of high ground to raise it to the level of the trucks and had no guide fence round it. When we tried to get the pigs inside, half of them went on to the line and, before we could do anything about it, a fast train roared by. The extraordinary thing was, that after it had passed and we looked to see what slaughter had been done, there was not a single casualty. We finally got the whole lot into the pen and so into the truck with the help of some of the railway men.

A pig can be one of the most dangerous animals on the farm, in fact I have heard a vet admit that it is the only animal of which he is afraid. It is astonishingly quick and its next move unpredictable, as anyone knows who has had a pig stand facing him, considering whether it would pass to left or right, or run between his legs. We had a particularly nasty sow to load one day and after several abortive attempts to get her where we wanted her, Joby, the lorry-driver said, 'Fetch me a bucket and a bit of meal.' When I brought the bucket, he got it over her eyes and backed her up the ramp into the van, 'as easy as spitting in your hand' was how one bystander described it. The old saying 'As ockerd as a pig,' is very apt; one farmer I knew, used to say, 'If you meet a pig, or a boy, give him a kick; if he's not coming from mischief, he's going to it.'

*　　*　　*

The Frogmarch

In the early days of the century, horse-power on the farm was just that. The horses were big, strongly-built animals, capable of dragging the plough through heavy land, or drawing loads of muck to the fields, or wagons of hay or corn from them. The only light horses about the place were generally more used to harness than the saddle and had little to do except take their master and mistress to market and home again, or the milk to the station.

A neighbour of mine, Bert Spencer, went to Gloucester every Saturday by train and bought half a dozen good geldings and packed them off to Draycott in charge of a drover, known to everyone as Harold. The horses were always very green, sometimes haltered for the first time only the day before, but there was usually one of the bunch more docile than the rest and this was chosen as leader. Harold would tie a halter round its neck, fasten the halter of Number 2 to it and so on till he had got them all in a string; then he would climb on the back of the leader and set out, arriving at Draycott in the early hours of the morning. Spencer's farm was only a small grass one, so homes had to be found for most of the horses at once. Bert's method was to lend them for a year to farmers who had a good horseman; at the end of the period three-year-olds would be four-year-olds and would have grown so much handier that, with luck, they were worth at least ten pounds more. I had a noted carter, some people would say a wagoner, and I usually had one or two of Spencer's horses in my team. There was no risk to me; they usually got fat and were in selling condition when they left me.

Spencer's best customers were the Railway Companies, the breweries and the big Corporations of which Manchester was one of the most important, but he had to do his business through a middle man, such as Tame of Stratford-upon-Avon, or Busby of Leicester. Busby, with his grey top hat and his mannerisms, was an outstanding figure at all the big horse Fairs, a wily old fox, who always had a sweetener in the form of a pair of gloves for a farmer's, or a dealer's wife. One year there was a painting of Stow Fair in the Royal Academy Exhibition and it was no trouble to pick him out among the crowd.

When I had what I thought was a good horse, I could not sell direct either to Busby or Tame—it had to go through Spencer's hands. Horse dealing was like the old rhyme:

Mr *Busby*
of *Leicester*

So, naturalists observe, a flea
Has smaller fleas that on him prey,
And these have smaller fleas to bite 'em,
And so proceed ad infinitum.

One rarely sees a draught horse nowadays, to the great impoverishment of the English scene, both rural and urban. Some of the large brewery firms still keep a few to advertise their product at agricultural shows and the like, but it must be increasingly difficult to find a matching team of Shires, Suffolks, or Clydesdales. I remember well a particularly fine grey Shire gelding that used to shunt the trucks up and down in Rugby station. My father loved to watch it work and one day, as he was waiting on the platform, he saw it go past drawing a truck; a few minutes later it was returning alone between the crowded platform and a stationary train drawn up on the opposite line, when a shrill whistle gave warning of the approach of an express. The horse realised that it was trapped, gave a terrified look round and made a tremendous leap on to the platform and there stood sweating and trembling as the train roared through the station on the line where it had been walking only seconds before. Surely this was a case of reasoning.

*   *   *

'*Have you seen any birds about?*' *a friend of mine once asked an old chap who worked on a shoot in which he had an interest.*

'*No, sir,*' *was the reply,* '*but I seen a 'nation great leathering bat last week!*'

33

CHAPTER SIX

The Three Hams—and Others

I HAD NOW SEEN the seasons pass over Neighbrook several times. Fields are as individual as people, each with its characteristics for good or bad, and I had now had opportunity to get to know those lying within my boundaries and could plan to put them to the best use. There was something to be learned even from their names— Fattening Cows Hill, Tump o' Trees Hill, Back Hill, Big Ploughed Field and Little Ploughed Field, Big Ham, Little Ham and Path Ham, Pool Ground, Rough Ground, Barn Ground and Coppice Ground, Fish Pond Field and the Slinget. But who was Joshua of Joshua's Meadow? No one could tell me that.

The three Hams—Ham, here, standing for meadow—lay along the Neighbrook and, like all the fields between the stream and Galloping Lane, on the ridge above, had a south aspect and were well sheltered from the north. Little Ham was directly in front of the house and was the best turf on the farm; I found my cows gave an extra ten gallons of milk a day when first turned into it and dropped back when moved to another field. I used to like to lie in bed and hear them grunting as they chewed the cud outside my window; actually they had all got indigestion from eating too much grass, but I never had a case of bloat.

deep ridge and furrow ploughing that is so characteristic of the Feldon district of Warwickshire. Different theories have been put forward as to its origin, the most feasible, to my mind, is that it is a legacy from the days of strip cultivation before the enclosures, when oxen were the draught animals. The headlands are very wide and drawn out at an angle to allow room for turning with a team of up to four beasts yoked abreast to a wooden beam; but in the Arden district, lying to the north of us, the ridges are much straighter because by the time it was cleared of woodland, horses were taking the place of oxen and the ploughs were much less cumbersome.

But whatever the history of those high ridges, they are a confounded nuisance. The only animal that crosses them with any grace is the fox; to gallop over them on horseback is no pleasure—but good for the liver—and with the coming of modern machinery many have disappeared. Some old farmers thought they gave a bigger acreage and I have heard a number of heated arguments on the subject; I remember there was one old gaffer who would not cut down his molehills, because he thought they gave him more land!

The ridges may serve a useful purpose on occasion, as one of my men confessed to me not long ago. Believing my predecessor at Weston Mill, where I now live, had gone out with his wife for the day, he thought—I expect it was April—that he would pop down and have a chat with the maid. He was boldly approaching the the front of the house over the ridge and furrow of the Dairy Ground, when he suddenly dropped flat on his tummy and crawled away in a deep furrow. My predecessor had not gone out after all and was standing at the front door!

Big Ham, like Little Ham, was another 'reaming good' grass field and I used to try to save it for spring grazing. An enormous elm grew by the water and first thing after every gale, I looked out to see if it were still standing, for it was isolated, without pro-

Like most of the fields on the farm, Little Ham was ribbed by the

tection from others, and had an enormous top with fourteen rooks' nests in it.

Path Ham, lying between Little Ham and my eastern boundary, was crossed by a right of way with a shaky plank bridge over the brook. It was a short cut between Stretton-on-Fosse and Aston Magna and was used daily by half a dozen men, working at the Aston Magna brickworks; several of them were members of the White family, all unusually big and strong and employed in timber-felling in the proper season. Fortunately for me, they were not averse to a little hay-loading if I was short-handed. There was a boggy patch in one corner of the field and I could not understand why the pigeons and doves came there to drink till I found that the water oozing up was brackish, which is much to the taste of the species. The brook had several good pools by Path Ham and one morning I found a trout, well over a pound in weight, on the bank where a heron had left it as being too big to swallow; there was a hole in the back where it had been struck, just to one side of the spine.

Joshua's Meadow, the only field I had on the far side of the brook, was of considerable interest to the naturalist in me. The flora included several uncommon flowers, bee-orchids among them, and meadow saffron, with its crocus-like blooms which appear in the early autumn after the leaves have died down. I shot my first snipe in Joshua's Meadow and more than once my little cocker spaniel, Sweep, flushed a water-rail from a ditchful of meadow sweet. On one notable occasion, as I drove past in a milk-float, it put up a smaller rail, which I took to be a Little Crake. I went back in the evening with my gun and when it got up from the same spot, I shot it. I thought it a triumph at the time—I was a trigger-happy youth—but I am not so sure about that now.

Until we made the road, there was no defined track across the meadow; one took one's own way over the turf and finding the bridge after dark could be a matter of guesswork. Edmund Gibbs, who had occupied Neighbrook some time before I did, was returning from Moreton with his wife one foggy, winter night in an old-fashioned, four-wheeled chaise, when the cob suddenly stopped and refused to go any further. The couple lost their nerve, knowing that there was a ten foot drop if they missed the bridge, and they unharnessed the horse, wrapped themselves in rugs and waited for the fog to lift; when it did they found themselves on the very edge of the brook. It was probably the sound of running water that had warned the horse not to go forward. Gibbs had worked several of the Ditchford and Blackdown farms as well as mine; he must have been something of an odd character, from the tales I have been told, one of which was that he only supplied sponge-cake and a bottle of pop for four o'clock tea!

*   *   *

During the twenty years I was at Neighbrook we experienced many floods over the fields bordering the brook and we had to be careful to move all livestock to higher ground in good time. The bridge linking Big Ham and Joshua's Meadow was sometimes three feet or more under water and then our only chance to get away from the farm was to go up to Galloping Lane and along the Fosse. I used to notice that if the wind blew upstream the water was much checked in subsiding, but if it blew downstream it pushed the water along a bit.

The brook was lined by a number of old willows. At one time they had been lopped, but the demand from the hurdle-makers fell and they were neglected and sprawled all over the place. Many had parasite plants growing out of their tops. A brown owl or two had their favourite tree where they could retreat from the rabble of small mobbing birds, and occasionally the moorhens nested in one of the crowns.

There were good trout, up to three pounds, in the brook, besides bullheads and minnows. Just below the bridge there was a deep pool which drained off into a shallow of small shingle and every spring the little lamperns, about four to six inches long, collected there to spawn. It was fascinating to see them moving quite large stones by picking them up with their suction apparatus and re-arranging them to their satisfaction, the while one or two trout waited below to catch any fish that strayed into deeper water. I found the lamperns were irresistible bait if spun on aerial tackle, and more than once I have waded up to them and caught one in my hand, fixed it on a flight and caught a good trout on it.

Another deadly bait was a wasp grub and these were to be had close at hand. The brook banks held a great attraction for the queens and, if we did not get a summer flood, the strong bikes that resulted were a menace to the angler, as they seemed to escape the badgers which scratched out those in the fields.

I once saw eels moving up stream, all of medium size, about a foot long, and there was often a big one under the bridge. Some of the species, of course, attain formidable length—and character! I remember, during a visit to Scotland, standing on the Crazy Bridge of Ayr and watching a diver being brought to the surface. I asked what he had been doing and was told he was filling in holes at the bottom of the pier. 'There are congers in some of them,' my informant added; 'the diver doesn't care about them much. He tried to dislodge an extra large one yesterday; it wouldn't budge and barked in his face, so he cemented it in!

Kingfishers brought off a brood of young in a hole in the bank below Joshua's Meadow and the otters must have had a holt near, but there was always the danger of being washed out in a storm. Unlike good little children, otters are more often heard than seen, and though they regularly worked the brook, I only caught sight of live ones twice. I was chatting with the signalman at Blockley station one day and he told me that when on night duty he often heard an otter come out of the culvert under the line and go splashing up the roadside ditch on its way to the lakes in Northwick Park.

Of course there were water rats—correctly speaking, water voles. The population varied; sometimes one might think there were none, at others they seemed to swarm, for, like their small cousins of the fields, they were subject to fluctuations. They were harmless creatures, except that they undermined the banks somewhat, but they used to annoy me when I was fishing by going to and fro in the water, generally with a blade of grass, or a mouthful of softer stuff for their nests. At such times the positioning of the eyes was very noticeable, set high in the head and so not submerged when the rat was swimming. They had need to keep a sharp lookout; stoats and weasels often decimated the colonies along the whole length of the brook, and I have no doubt the heron took its toll—I saw one heron in a flooded field catch and swallow a mole, so a water-rat would not be an unmanageable mouthful. My little dog Teazle found the rats provided plenty of sport; he never caught any to my knowledge, but once, after a furious dig, he produced a water-shrew.

I tried to improve the brook by placing staddle stones across to form two little waterfalls, but the current was much too strong and they were soon swept away.

.   .   .

Four large fields climbed the slope between the Hams and Galloping Lane—Tump o' Trees Hill and Pool Ground, and above them Bottom of Back Hill and Fattening Cows Hill.

Tump o' Trees Hill was immediately above the farm premises, a cone-shaped field of forty-odd acres with a cluster of old ash trees in the middle that had been pollarded at some time and then left to grow again. There were more ashes in one of the hedges and these held a considerable rookery. On the whole it was a useful field, but uneven; good turf on the part that sloped to the south, poor on that which faced north.

Pool Ground, lying side by side with Tump o' Trees Hill, deserves special mention for the enormous crop of hay it grew one year. The large pond from which it took its name was interesting. Wild duck dropped in there at night and provided an occasional meal for the household, and many migrant and water-loving birds made it a port of call; I have seen a greenshank, common and green sandpipers, coot, moorhens, and, sometimes, a heron after frogs. The greenshank, the only one I had seen this side of the Border, arrived about midsummer and stayed till Michaelmas. It had a quick take-off and a wild call; if disturbed it flew over Tump o' Trees Hill to Blakemoor Pool half a mile to the north, and, if startled there, it flew back to me—it was always to be found on the edge of one or other sheet of water.

Bottom of Back Hill also had a pond, but only of interest to thirsty stock.

Fattening Cows Hill was one of the best fields on the farm, as could be inferred from its name, forty acres of old turf in high ridge and furrow, just as the ox-team had left it long ago. It gave two tons of hay to the acre in a growing season and, being exposed, the grass dried easily after cutting; as most of it faced south, there was often a bit of 'early bite' in it. It had one fault; there was only a small pond, not big enough for so large an area.

A dreadfully rough, rutty road led from the farm buildings through Tump o' Trees Hill and Fattening Cows Hill to Galloping Lane and we used it to haul muck to the arable fields beyond. It had its uses, for we broke in several young horses on it, but it killed a too-willing mare which died from a twisted gut. I nearly came to grief on it myself the latter part of my occupation of the farm, when I had abandoned a horse and trap in favour of a car. There was an inch or two of snow on the ground and driving home I thoughtlessly applied the brakes and found myself tobogganing down Fattening Cows Hill at an ever-increasing rate. It was some experience! I suppose we should have done well to improve the track, but we never did; long after we left, my successor made a stone road across the two fields.

The fields on the far side of Galloping Lane fell away to the north, which was of no advantage except in a drought when a little grass would still grow on this cooler slope, while it was all burnt up on the south-facing one; there was the added snag that the area was out of sight of the house and farm buildings behind Tump o'

Trees Hill and crows, rooks, rabbits and the rest took full advantage of the situation. There were many more rooks then than there are now and it was a sight on a winter's evening to see them fly over to their communal roost at Northwick Park. I think the carrion crow did more damage per bird but they did not congregate so much, each pair being very jealous of its particular territory, even in the non-breeding season. I never had to complain about serious loss caused by game, though there was enough about to provide a good day's shoot; pigeons were not the menace they are nowadays but rabbits swarmed.

Barn Ground was one of Neighbrook's worst rabbit-infested fields, but it was useful all the same, for the barn that gave it its name had a yard and ample water. Old Thomas Beesley used to spend the winter up there, his main job looking after a bunch of cattle and foddering them night and morning. The yard gate was left open and they ran out in Fishpond Field during the day; they always did well under his care and went away without any check when the grass came in the spring, in fact, as the old farmers used to say, they met it. His spare time was spent hedging and ditching, not too far away, for he was getting old and stiff. I enjoyed helping him for an hour sometimes, cutting out the big pieces and giving him a hand with a bit of draining. There was one place where the roots of the willows got into the pipes, forming a long rope inside and completely blocking them, and we had to dig them up and clear them every two or three years. Beesley was a fine old fellow, always tidy, one of nature's gentlemen. He worked for me for several years, then he slipped on a ladder and barked his shin, the wound would not heal and was the main cause of his death when nearly eighty.

Barn Ground was a very quiet and peaceful spot and the foxes from Blakemoor Cover often had a comfortable sleep in the manger. It is very different to-day; it has all been modernised and grain-driers and the like have replaced the old buildings which had survived for hundreds of years.

41

South of Barn Ground was Top of Back Hill. A solitary ruin of an old crab tree stood in the middle, and here I saw, or, should I say, heard my first Little Owl: it was early spring and it was making full use of its banshee call. Westwards were Little Ploughed Field of no particular memory, and Big Ploughed Field where I learnt to drive a tractor; while to the north of Barn Ground and bordering the Paddle Brook, was Fish Pond Field, a very difficult place to harvest. In the very wet summer of 1911 we spent eleven weeks trying to make hay there. I had previously manured the ground with dung and a chemical mixture called Limphos; it had been a growing season and we cut over two tons to the acre, but we could not get it dried and in the end we had to take the black stuff, that ought to have been hay, off the ground in muck-carts, otherwise it would have killed the grass underneath. The weather cleared up later and eventually I got a lot of good hay, and though it was lacking in June buttercups, it was so full of white clover that the stock went for it 'good and hearty.'

The pool that gave the field its name was on the far side of the Paddle Brook; it went with the Blackdowns Farm and was not part of my property, but I was allowed to fish and shoot there. It was a picturesque spot, about an acre in extent, with a foreground of giant mace, which some people call bulrushes, and an island reached by a single-plank bridge; the background was woodlands, including a round coppice of fir-trees. It was so isolated and quiet that there was always the chance of seeing something unusual. Wild duck and teal came in at night and I remember a Mandarin drake, evidently an escapee from somebody's ornamental lake. Water-rail nested in the rushes and made one jump by the extraordinary noises they made; herons and kingfishers were often to be found, but the Loch Leven trout were too big for the former and they had to be content with frogs. I have seen passing peregrines—my shepherd's name for them was 'they big grey 'awks'—take a moorhen from the water, a bird easy to catch and to which predators are partial. I was up there one evening when a dozen larks, or pippits swished over my head, followed by a cock sparrow-hawk. They kept in a compact flock until they were half way across Fish Pond Field and then one panicked, or could not keep up the pace, and in a second it was seized.

On another evening, watching a nightjar flying backwards and forwards as I waited with my gun by a dead tree near the pool, a Great Spotted woodpecker suddenly poked its head out of a hole above me; it was the first I had ever seen, though the Lesser nested in two places on the farm and the Green was fairly common. Locally the latter is known as the Eccle. If I had not already realised why it was so named, I could have been in no doubt after hearing one calling loudly in alarm as it was being chased by a sparrowhawk round and round an ivy-covered tree. I could not be sure of the outcome, but I think it made good its escape.

The pool had been stocked with a few hundred trout which turned cannibal, the bigger ones preying on the smaller till there were only about a dozen large fish left. A little girl, fishing from the island with a dead bluebottle, caught one of eight-and-a-half pounds. The others went down the brook when the weir gave way; I happened to go that way one evening soon afterwards and it was amazing to see those huge trout leaping out of the water after mayfly. There was not a sign of fish in the pool for some years following and it was a very dead piece of water.

The two fields on my western boundary between Galloping Lane and the Paddle Brook were Ewe Ground and Rough Ground. Ewe Ground was a favourite place for hares when there were no sheep there, perhaps because the herbage contained a lot of bed-straw, both white and yellow. I never discovered how the field got its name; it was unsuitable for lambing, as it had no pen and was far from any building; but there could be no doubt why Rough Ground was so called, it was all humps and hollows, with anthills that would fill the bed of a dung-cart, and a covert of gorse and thorn that often held a fox. I shot my first woodcock there; it fell in a thick place and I spent a long time retrieving it, groping about on hands and knees on the prickly ground, while all the time it was suspended from the top of a gorse bush with its wings spread. I cut a wide ride up the middle of the gorse covert in order to get on better terms with the rabbits, but one had to be quick!

Between Rough Ground and Fish Pond Field, were Coppice Ground, with a group of ash trees where pigeons roosted, and a narrow field generally alluded to as the Slinget. It was along the bottom of the Coppice that I met a vixen, heavy in whelp, carrying a rabbit; she almost walked up to me as I stood perfectly still in her path. There was a fox earth just over my boundary in Alfred Longford's sand-pit and this was where she had her cubs.

CHAPTER SEVEN

The Four Shires Stone

ABOUT FOUR MILES south-west of Neighbrook and a good mile out
of Moreton-in-Marsh on the Chipping Norton road stands the
Four Shires Stone, once marking the meeting place of four county
boundaries, Warwickshire, Worcestershire, Gloucester and Oxford. I have had many a good day's shooting in its neighbourhood
and a party of us once accounted for forty brace of partridge between two o'clock and six. It was one of my ambitions to stand in
one county, shoot a right and left at partridges driven from a second
and retrieve one from each of the remaining two. I only did it
once and no one can repeat the performance now, for the isolated
splinter of Worcestershire that once touched the monument has
been transferred to Gloucestershire in which it was embedded.

Though the present stone is comparatively modern, there seems
to have been one on the site for many hundreds of years; old documents refer to it as the Scoerston. Back in 1016, when I imagine
the area round about was little more than a scrubby heath of birches
bracken and brambles, it was the scene of one of those indecisive
skirmishes between the Saxons and the Danes; in later times it
witnessed battles of another type, for when bare-knuckle contests
were made illegal, it became the favourite rendezvous for prize-
fights in the old style. If the police from one county arrived on the

45

scene, having got wind of what was happening, belligerents and onlookers alike, instead of taking to their heels, stepped across the boundary out of the jurisdiction of that particular force and went on with their sport! I was told by a farmer friend that when a boy he rode in front of his father to see a fight at the Stone. The saddle was a good vantage point as they looked over the heads of the spectators on foot—and were not so likely to have their pockets picked!

Although my land was surrounded by Gloucestershire, it was actually situated in one of the many isolated islands of Worcester-shire that complicated administration in the neighbourhood of the Stone until fairly recently, and when I received a notice to renew my dog licence in the County in which I resided—the money went to the relief of the rates—I put it on one side to await a convenient time to make a special journey to Shipston-on-Stour, and forgot it! Then, of course, I had to make the trip, convenient or not, and answer for my sin of omission. I pleaded guilty and explained how it had happened, but unfortunately I was the first on the list of some thirty other defaulting dog-owners. In an aside to the Clerk to the Justices, which I was not supposed to hear, the Chairman of the Magistrates suggested, 'There's a good deal in what he says'; but the Clerk replied, 'If we let him off, what about all the rest of them?' and we were all fined seven-and-six per dog—£1.2.6 for me and half a day lost.

There were disadvantages in living near the Four Shires Stone!

Not only must the sportsman have a licence for his dog and his gun and his trap, he must also possess one to allow him to kill game. I have an old licence hanging on the wall of the little room I call my gun-room; it is dated 1846 and cost four pounds and ten-pence. Nowadays its counterpart costs six guineas, or its equivalent in decimal currency, a very modest increase in a hundred-and-twenty-odd years; but it is astonishing what a lot of people manage to evade it and what a lot of game is killed every season without the gun-owner having paid a penny! In the whole of my long shooting career I have only been asked once to show my licence. It was when I was a very young man, out with a large Boxing-Day party of farmers and horse-dealers, on some of whom, the local constable, a rather officious individual, had a 'down.' We were standing round a rabbit bury that was being stirred up by a couple of ferrets when he arrived and I believe only myself and one other possessed the correct papers; the rest had just the ordinary ten-shilling gun-licence, with a single exception, a horse-dealer, who had no papers at all! While the constable was doing his duty and taking names and addresses, the arch defaulter propped his gun against a rick and was calmly lighting his pipe when the officer of the law got round to him. The bluff succeeded and he was passed over without a question being asked!

In the days before myxomatosis almost wiped out the rabbit population, poaching was much more lucrative than it is now, and a good many people must have profited at my expense, for the north side of my farm was one big warren to the detriment of farm stock. Perhaps I ought to have been grateful to the uninvited pest-controllers and it was certainly much easier to turn a blind eye than take any action, but there was a limit to my patience. A particular gang of gypsies frequently camped in the middle of my farm in Galloping Lane and as far as I could see, they lived on the proceeds of poaching my rabbits and the sale of clothes-pegs made from ash cut from my fences. They took the same advantage of divided civil authority as the prize-fighters used to do, only going a few hundred yards into the next Shire when moved on by the police, and coming back if warned off the new pitch. I tolerated them for a long time, but when I found they had turned their horses at night into my best fields and had milked three of my cows in the early hours one morning, it seemed high time to do something. They knew as well as I did that, if I took out a summons, no amount of boundary skipping would be of any use and they departed in a hurry and never returned.

I was lucky that they did not attempt retaliation, for the hardened poacher generally shows his resentment of interference in some unpleasant manner. When I was a boy, living on the outskirts of Leamington, the police, without consulting my father, hid in our garden to waylay some poachers returning with their catch. We were disturbed in the middle of the night by a confused shouting and learnt later that several men were caught with their nets and a score or more of rabbits, but that some of the gang got away. My father had a special pen of Silver Wyandottes, of which he was inordinately proud, and a night or two later they disappeared— all except one that roosted out! We always thought they had been taken in the belief that my father had something to do with the arrest, and our suspicions were strengthened when the fowl were found some weeks later buried in sacks in a nearby coppice.

It was about that same time, for I remember Brabner was Chief Constable of Leamington, a gang of poachers was caught trying to smuggle a bag of thirty-odd rabbits into the town. When the Superintendent asked Brabner what he should do with the car- cases, he was told, 'Oh, give them to the men, but keep the skins!' I think it worked out at a rabbit for each constable and two for the sergeants.

It was warm weather and in the interval before the case came up, the very astute lawyer for the defence, Crowther Davis, got to know of what had happened and at the hearing he demanded the rabbits should be produced in Court. When the bundle of stinking skins was brought in, the judge was so annoyed that he dismissed the case and the poachers enjoyed a period of compara- tive peace from the police for some time!

Game poaching needs more organisation than picking up the few rabbits, for the keeper must be taken into account. Several of us once drove a considerable distance to take part in a drive and as we walked a sunny, bracken ridge bare, I heard a young keeper say regretfully, 'I can't understand it! The bank was all of a charm with birds last week!'—and he was not referring to goldfinches. One of the beaters confided to me that the young fellow was a bit too fond of the local and some of the village poachers would arrange to keep him there till closing time, while the rest made a raid on the game.

A friend of mine had better luck—and not due to an absence of poachers; he told me he went on a shoot in Norfolk and actually ran out of cartridges! The party sat down to lunch near an outlying covert and the keeper had just said that they were only likely to get an odd bird or two, when they saw about a score of pheasants cross one of the rides. They got, not a bird or two, but seventy! They learnt the reason later. The Nabob, who had rented the adjoining shoot, had turned down a hundred hand-reared pheasants in readiness for the following week when he was expecting several V.I.P.'s for a day's sport and the birds, being new to the ground, had wandered too far afield and crossed the boundary.

The poaching I resented most was on that mile of trout stream, the Neighbrook, which was my pride and delight, and when I was strolling along the bank one Sunday evening and a little bit of paper speared on a thorn caught my eye, I was instantly suspicious. It could hardly have got there accidentally and seeing another piece speared on the next thorn bush, and then another and another, I cut a long willow stick with a hooked end and fished about in the water wherever tell-tale markers appeared and collected a dozen night-lines. None of them had a fish on, but the worms on the hooks were all chewed up. There was very little stream where the lines were set and more coarse fish than trout, but the trout were 'regular sockdolagers' and it was no doubt for these that the lines had been so hopefully set.

I went back to the spot a day or two later and found a groom hunting the bank with some terriers.

'Keep those dogs up!' I ordered. 'Someone has been setting night-lines down here and I should like to know who it was!'

I never found another line, but I wonder if my veiled threat did more than make him avoid my reach of the brook when he had a taste for trout. An old farmer told me how he had been cured of poaching. A number of pheasants roosted on the ground in some thick rushes on his farm, and he got up very early one morning, thinking he would get a brace of them without anyone being the wiser. Luck was with him and he got a right and left at a pheasant and a hare. 'Very neatly done, young man!' said a voice just behind him and there was his landlord!

No threats, no recriminations, but the erring tenant never poached again.

When I knew him he owned seven-hundred acres of land which he had formerly rented and I have had many a good day's sport there and shot more than one snipe at the very spot where the old boy had poached his hare and pheasant half a century before.

The divided authority of the law in the neighbourhood of the Four Shires Stone was matched by divided authority of the local hunts. Neighbrook was in a neutral zone; the North Cotswolds hunted it for the first month or two of the season and the Warwickshire for the rest, an arrangement, I regret to say, that led to some jealousy. In a fox-hunting country, every earth is known and the young are reared in security till suitably thinned out by cubbing, and some of the keen Warwickshire men would have it that the North Cotswold killed too many. The North Cotswold retaliated by accusing the Warwickshire of improving sport for themselves by sending in an occasional bagman. Of course this illegality was denied, but but after a fox had gone away from one of my small covers, I found a bag stuffed in a rabbit hole; there was sandy soil, unlike ours, in it, and some fox hairs and an unmistakeable foxy smell!

The most important question for the farmer was which Hunt was responsible for settling poultry claims and repairing fences.

The North Cotswold built a very good bridge over the Paddle Brook where it formed my northern boundary; it led from Blackdown into Pool Ground, but it was too narrow to admit more than one horseman at a time, a handicap with which I had no quarrel, my sympathies being on the side of the fox. If a fox got away from that point it usually meant a good run as there was no other cover nearer than Northwick Park, unless towards Aston Hale.

The Neighbrook was a formidable obstacle for the horseman, too wide to jump and not easy to ford. There was a shaky, single-planked bridge from Path Ham over the water, and that thruster, Victor Cartright, who had the reputation of being the boldest horseman in England, once rode across it and had the hounds to himself for miles. I have heard that Lord Portman, when he was Master of the Warwickshire, jumped the brook—perhaps I should say, got across it!

❊   ❊   ❊

An old friend of mine used to pay an annual visit to Sutton-Scotney for three days, partridge shooting. It was before the days of motor cars and he was met at the station by an old ostler. Their route took them past a large house in process of being built, but my friend could not see that any additions had been made since his last year's visit. 'What is the owner's name?' he asked. 'I'm not sure, sir,' replied the ostler, 'but I did see something about it in the local paper and if I remember rightly it was Mr Assets Nil.'

CHAPTER EIGHT

Noyfull Fowles and Vermin

'TO PLOUGH AND SOW, and reap and mow,' is not all that goes to the making of a farmer's boy or, more particularly, of a farmer, for the crops must be protected from what an Act of Elizabeth I dubs 'Noyfull Fowles and Vermyn.' A previous Act under Henry VIII obliged every parish, township and hamlet to provide itself with a net for catching crows, rooks and choughs and placed a price on their heads of twopence a dozen, the cost to be met by the landowners. It would seem these gentlemen did not play their part, for under Elizabeth the duty of collecting the money, inspecting the kill and paying the killer devolved on the Church Wardens. It is noticeable that in the thirty years intervening between the two Acts, the pay had doubled and the heads of three old crows were valued at a penny.

In the latter half of the eighteenth century the Church Warden's account book for the tiny parish of Sutton-under-Brailes, some five miles east of Neighbrook, shows that amounts varying from seven shillings to thirteen-and-sixpence were paid in some years for 'sparrows, snakes and urchins,' the spelling being as variable as the sums' total. Comparison with other entries of the period indicate that it was easy money. In 1768, Matthew Jellyman charged only fourteen shillings for five new bell-ropes—Sutton church has only five bells to this day; while Mary Pigeon got no more than sixpence for the backaching job of 'lading Water out of the Church'. Two years later, Thomas of the same name, received double that sum for 'Caren the water out of the Church in a Flood'—is this an early example of unequal pay for equal work?

One of the troubles of pest control is that the damning title of 'vermin' is often given on no better ground than superstition, or supposition. The snake's chief offence seems to be that it has no legs; and why should the slaughter of hedgehogs be encouraged when they live almost exclusively on slugs and maggots and the like? As for owls, what more vigilant Rodent Officers, alias Rat-Catchers, could we have? One year when there was a plague of field mice and voles, a pair of short-eared owls nested just over my boundary and on a summer evening they would soar like buzzards on the thermal currents; sometimes they were joined by others and there would be half a dozen of them together, though normally we never saw one till winter had set in.

As a farmer my chief reason for considering the sparrow a *Noyfull Fowle* is that, after rearing several broods of youngsters in the villages and small towns, he takes his annual holiday in the country and starts to devour the standing crops, working round from the edges of a field till there is little grain left on the headlands. Before the first World War the farms in South Warwickshire were mostly grass with a little arable ground round the stedding and this so concentrated the sparrows that farmers and allotment holders were driven to plant bearded wheat, which to some extent defeated the marauders.

It was once common practice to employ boys to frighten the birds from the corn and keep them on the move with various noisy contraptions, but it only sent the pillagers from one part of the field to another. I can remember when roosting sparrows were caught by gangs of youths using a bat-fowling net, an affair something like a double lacrosse net that folded in the middle. Half the party would go down one side of a big hedge, while the rest walked along the other with a lantern held behind the raised net, and as the hedge was tapped the birds fluttered towards the light and were trapped. I do not think the number of sparrows was reduced to any

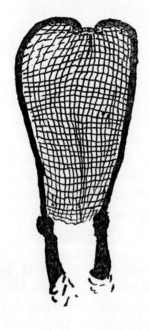

Bat-fowling net closed

appreciable extent, but those that were caught made a very tasty pie. Unfortunately, felts and other thrushes, and an occasional rarity, fell victim to the hunt and I remember a ring ousel being taken in one of my hedges—or was it a blackbird with a white feather or two?

The farmer is not the sparrows' only enemy; predators, themselves classed as vermin by gamekeepers, find small birds a palatable meal. I have seen sparrow-hawks kill a number of times and usually it is but a matter of seconds, but one morning when I was discussing some business with my hay-merchant just by the house, a hen killed at our very feet. She was so intent on the chase that she had not seen us and I had time to notice that she had her beak open and was panting for breath; she must have curved her wings forward to impede her victim, for she had gripped several of her own wing-feathers along with it. Before she flew off, the Little Musket, or cock, settled for one second on a pale in a gap in the fence, showing that they were hunting together; their youngsters were clamouring for breakfast in an old carrion crow's nest close by.

But in spite of everything, the sparrow remains as ubiquitous as ever. Perhaps it is as well. Some two hundred years ago that wise man, Frederick II of Prussia, afterwards called The Great, offered a per capita reward to the slayers of the sparrows that plagued his orchards and ravaged his people's fields. He soon discovered the danger of indiscriminate destruction, for the crops began to suffer from swarms of caterpillars and he had to reverse his earlier policy and offer a reward for every pair of sparrows introduced into the country.

The delicate balance of nature is not to be upset lightly. Charles Darwin pointed out the connection between cats and a good clover crop; the bumble-bee fertilises the clover, but its nest is destroyed by the long-tailed field mouse, which, in its turn, is the prey of cats; therefore, fewer cats, more mice. What chance then have the bees to survive in sufficient numbers to play their part in seed production?

It has been suggested that the present disturbing increase in the number of wood-pigeons is in some measure due to the scarcity of squirrels. Foresters and gamekeepers have tried to discredit them by calling them Tree Rats and have hunted them ruthlessly, consequently the pigeon's eggs, on which they delighted to feast, have been left to hatch.

Wood pigeons are a far greater threat to the farmer than sparrows, for they will attack every sort of green crop and congregate in such large flocks that I have known them completely strip a promising field of young clover in a few days; what is more, they are with us all the year round. I have shot hundreds from the coppice between Big Ploughed Field and Coppice Ground. When there was snow about I used to wear my white cow-gown, which was not only warm, but a wonderful camouflage.

Crows and rooks are other birds that are generally classed as vermin, but undeservedly, though they can do a lot of damage while making themselves useful. I used to go to some trouble to drive them away, but a scarecrow, or mawkin as they are called about here, has little effect once it has become a familiar object in a field. The best thing, I found, was to shoot a rook or two, cut off the heads and fix them with the beaks pointing skywards as though the bodies were buried. A lot of mixed corvines would soon collect and fly round and round above, cawing, but they would not settle in that part of the field for some time. One year the crows made such a determined attack on a newly-drilled field of spring corn that I gave in and decided to leave them alone. I was rewarded by a good crop; the crows were after wire-worms and not my seed; but to withstand such pest control, drilling must not be too shallow, or the young seedlings will be pulled up with the leather-jackets, wire-worms, or whatever is destroying the roots.

Rabbits were the worst pests at Neighbrook. I have shot many a one as it tried to cross a narrow field we called the Slinget, beyond Path Ham, and they offered sporting shots, particularly in Pool

"Familiarity breeds contempt."

Ground, as they crossed the high ridge and furrow. They would jump out of their forms at one's feet, too near to shoot, and disappear over the opposite ridge into the trough beyond, to reappear for a brief second on the next ridge, not at the point where one expected them, but a yard or two to the right or left. I have seen many a good shot humiliated by them. We used to stink them out and get a party to deal with them and we often shot over two hundred in a day; it was very good sport with odds on the rabbit. I used to let the guns have what they wanted and then take the rest in the boot of the car to Mr Barnes of Shipston; he took them to Coventry, where there was a ready market. He was a good payer and settled each week for those he had had the week before. At that time the pelts were worth as much as the carcases; I have forgotten how many he told me he could skin in an hour, but it was fantastic and reminded me of when, as a schoolboy, I was allowed sometimes to peep behind the scenes of the big poulterer's shop in Leamington and watch expert pluckers at work; their speed was amazing, less than three minutes per bird.

When I was first farming, not far from Leamington, thinking to make a little profit while trying to safeguard my corn, I rashly engaged those notorious poachers, who did odd jobs for my father, Beefy and Chang, to catch rabbits for me with a long net. I had not reckoned on them trying to follow their 'vocation' under my very nose! I met them at the appointed place at 11 p.m. and must confess I got quite a thrill counting the rabbits as I heard them running over the crisp, frozen grass and into the net. But after we had caught several score and reached the boundary of my land, it appeared to be high time to dismiss my assistants, for there, drawn up out of the moonlight under a big hedge, I spotted a small pony and trap in charge of two strangers—strangers to me, but not to Beefy and Chang, I suspect!

I might have turned my worst rabbit-ridden fields to account by selling turf. The finest turf for golf greens used to be cut from warrens where the constant gnawing and nibbling had killed off the coarser weeds and grasses; in fact, a very good way to improve an old lawn is to pen rabbits over it on very small wire-mesh, the smallness preventing scratching. Since myxamatosis, turf suitable for greens costs the earth, sometimes it seems to be worth more than the freehold!

Like grey squirrels and little owls, rabbits are not natives, and we might have been spared much loss and trouble if someone had not had the idea of introducing some from Spain in 1200; before the century was out, they had already become so plentiful that it is recorded that two thousand skins were exported in one year from Lundy Island alone.

Mimi catches a weasel.

CHAPTER NINE

The—Sometimes—Aggressive—Male

THE MOST AMUSING bull story I know was told me by an old friend, Mrs Michael Bennett of Long Compton. The car park near the station at Oxford was formerly the cattle market and she remembers her father sending a fat bull there to be sold and the sensation it caused. It was led into the town on a pole and when it reached the neighbourhood of the market, the stockman in charge tied it to some strong iron railings and slipped into a nearby inn for a quick one. He returned in a few minutes, wiping his mouth, and stood aghast—the bull had vanished! Then his attention was caught by a crowd of people gazing up at the first story of a china shop; he looked up too and there was the bull calmly surveying the scene through a plate-glass window! Left alone and dazed and puzzled by its unusual surroundings, it had managed to free itself, as bulls often do, and had wandered through the open doors of the shop, up the wide staircase and along the aisle between the shelves of crockery as far as the window. Fortunately it was a quiet old thing and made no fuss when the stockman came up talking soothingly, and it allowed itself to be taken by the ring in its nose and led downstairs and back into the market-place. Unlike the proverbial bull in a china shop, it did no damage except to sweep an odd cup to the floor with its tail.

As a rule bulls do not deserve their reputation for aggressiveness, but if two of them happen to meet, a trial of strength is almost sure to follow. Sheer weight and muscle do not always carry the day. One of my neighbours had a young Ayrshire bull that was inclined to trespass on adjoining farms and during one of these jaunts it encountered a Hereford, twice its weight and size, which had the additional advantage of being on its home ground. But the Ayrshire was active and used its grey matter. They met on a steep bank and the little fellow contrived to keep on the higher ground so that while he was thrusting downwards, his opponent had to fight an uphill battle and was only too glad to break off and retreat with what dignity it could command.

Like bulls, rams are aggressive when they first meet and, again, it is not always the bigger one that wins. I was my own flockmaster for one period at Neighbrook and I used to grease the rams' heads; this was specially important after shearing, as animals that had been lying peacefully together before being relieved of their fleeces, often failed to recognise each other in the nude. They would back away, twenty feet or more, and then rush head on with a horrible thud. Not infrequently one of the combatants had its neck broken by the impact; but animals that had had their foretops made slippery with grease generally escaped serious injury, though a short-legged ram could dislocate the neck of a taller one because the blow came below the centre of gravity.

It seems inevitable with most animals that the question of mastery must be decided before they can live peaceably together. One of my neighbours, Stephen Mumford, at the end of each travelling season, used to remove the shoes from half a dozen entire horses and turn them out for the winter in a strongly-fenced paddock; there they would face up to each other and fight with their forefeet and teeth, only using their heels for a parting shot. As soon as one had become master, they settled down together like a flock of sheep.

I have seen dog foxes fight on several occasions; no holds are barred and the fur certainly flies; I think the same applies to badgers, but I have only the evidence of my ears in this case, as the battles usually take place under cover of darkness—the noise is exactly like that of angry pigs.

One evening when waiting for a large trout to rise again to a mayfly, I had proof that, contrary to the general belief, rabbits use their teeth in fighting. An old rabbit suddenly appeared at the top of the opposite bank, then halted in a listening attitude. A moment later, a yard below and half way down the bank, two more old rabbits came struggling out of a hole, the one holding the other by the back with its teeth! The one being ejected looked scared and was doing its best to get away and, when the hold suddenly gave, he was catapulted with a splash into the brook, putting my trout down for that evening!

Cocks will fight to the death and cock-fighting, no longer permitted, goes back to ancient days; Asia has the credit, or dis-credit, for first fostering it. In Edward III's reign the sport was so fashionable that there was a royal cockpit. London's Cockspur Street takes it name from the silver spurs that used to be made there and a few old cockpits are still to be found; one at Fell Mill is only a few miles upstream from Shipston-on-Stour.

I am afraid the human male is just as ready to resent intrusion and insult as the lesser ceration. The elderly folk of a certain Cotswold village not many miles from Neighbrook still tell with a chuckle of a somewhat hot-tempered villager who, hearing that a derogatory remark had been made about a member of his family in a local pub, marched straight to the churchyard where the defamer was digging a grave and invited him to come out and take a good hiding. The invitation was declined, the nature of the hole and its situation on consecrated ground seemed to offer asylum, but the wrathful one was not going to let considerations of propriety delay punishment and he jumped into the hole to administer it. I have forgotten which of the combatants climbed out the victor, but I think they must both have found their style considerably cramped.

I think it was an old fellow from the same village who, nursing some grudge against his next-door neighbour, refused to soil his lips with the offender's name and always alluded to him as 'he by we.'

CHAPTER TEN

Old Ways and New

A KEEN YOUNG FELLOW called Holcroft, wanting to gain experience, once came to me for a temporary job. After he had been at Neighbrook for a couple of months, he went to one of my neighbours, whose name was not, but should have been, Bacchus, an outstandingly good farmer, but a heavy drinker.

On Holcroft's first day, his new master, exceedingly drunk, was brought home from market by his foreman, in a milkfloat drawn by a fast, high-mettled cob. The farm, like mine, stood back from the road across several fields and an argument broke out as to which of the men should get down and open the intervening gates; the foreman was reluctant to trust his master with the reins, but he had to do it in the end, for Bacchus refused to leave his seat. Nothing untoward happened till the last gate was being closed. It was at that moment that Bacchus chose to give the cob a cut with the whip, which it certainly did not require; it immediatley bolted for home and at the sharp turn into the farmyard the cart was tipped upside down, pinning Bacchus under it and throwing the cob on its side. Holcroft was feeding some pigs nearby and ran to the animal's head as it lay kicking, but Bacchus, peering drunkenly through the side of the float, swore at him in no measured terms and ordered him back to work!

About a week later, just as I was going to bed, Holcroft knocked at the door and asked if I could put him up for the night; Bacchus had come home drunk again and kicked him out and he was too frightened to return. I gave the lad a bed and next morning, in spite of my remonstrances, he went straight off and took out a summons aganist his master for assault. The effect on that festive soul was very sobering, for he was desperately afraid of the matter reaching the ears of his landlord, and he came straight over and begged me to use my influence to get the summons withdrawn. I asked what he was prepared to do and he said he was ready to apologise and pay five pounds damages. Holcroft jumped at the offer, and as he pocketed the fiver, he turned to Bacchus with, 'You can do it again as often as you like on the same terms!'

Whether Holcroft got tired of being kicked, or was not kicked enough, I do not know, but a few months later I got a letter from him in western Canada, where he was finding plenty of new jobs to tackle.

As for Bacchus, he met with a serious accident soon afterwards, trying to gallop the cob down a very steep hill in Aston Magna with a bend and a stone wall at the bottom. He finished up with a hole in his head. The doctor told me he put three fingers into the opening in an effort to find a piece of skull; he never expected the patient to live, but he did, to work—and drink—as hard as ever.

It was no fault of Bacchus that this was the first accident he had caused on that particular hill, for I knew a sober farmer who was forced to gallop his own horse down it to escape Bacchus hard behind him, singing a ribald song at the top of his voice!

Farmers thereabouts seemed to be tough, for another neighbour of mine had an extraordinary accident, also with a horse. He was doing a little amateur veterinary work, docking some colts, when one of them lashed out and caught him on the chin. That would have been unpleasant enough by itself, but as he was holding his tongue between his teeth at the time, a habit he had when doing a particularly ticklish job, he bit the end clean off! He was nearly choked by the remainder of the tongue swelling and he was not able to speak for months; indeed it was feared he would be dumb for life and so he might have been were he not such a determined fellow. His wife told me he would go out into the farmyard and lean over a sty and make queer noises at the pigs in an effort to regain his speech. He succeeded so well that from where I lived, at least a mile away, I could often hear him 'talking' to his men!

There are arguments for and against docking. I have more than once been obliged to lean over the dashboard of a dogcart to release a rein from beneath the tightly tucked-down, undocked tail of a youngster, no enviable task if it is doing its best to kick the trap to bits, or bolt! On the other hand I nearly came to grief one day through a dock being too short.

Warwickshire hounds had met at Long Compton and I had pushed my cycle up to the top of Harrow Hill, from which one could see for miles into the Heythrop country, only to find hounds had turned into Weston Park. I was thinking of abandoning my

machine and following on foot, when Cecil Cox drove up in a smart, new turn-out which he had bought only the day before at Cheltenham Repository—now no more. He invited me to jump up beside him and, nothing loth, I did so and we went spanking over the bouncy turf of the hill, the brand-new harness squeaking for want of use. The dog cart was on the high side and could easily have been turned over, but all went well and we gained the hard road. Hounds had worked towards Whichford Wood and, half-way down Stourton Hill we were beginning to wonder if we were going away from them, when a fox crossed the road in front of us. Cox tried to pull up, but the road was so steep that the cob put his feet together and started to slither! I could see the crupper climbing up the cob's absurdly short dock until it slipped right over. The harness had no breeching, which normally takes the weight and thrust from behind; there was only a kicking strap and the tail-board hit the rump of the cob, nearly catapulting both of us over its head. A good thing Cox was big and strong and the harness new! He managed to pull up and I was just able to get to the cob's head as the hounds came thundering by in full cry!

I have done docking in my time, but it is far from the pleasantest job about the farm and generally I have been only too happy to leave it and like surgery to the trained hands of the vet—in my case, Will Walker, senior and junior. In the old days veterinary surgeons were few and it took time to get hold of one, while there was generally some unqualified person in the neighbourhood who pro-fessed to know a bit about farriery. My father often told the tale of the pet donkey he used to ride as a small boy. One day it was taken ill and the village sweep, the local quack, was called in. The case was really beyond his skill, but he examined the animal, played for safety and, diagnosing it to be suffering from colic, prescribed a 'ball.' He was in the act of administering the remedy by putting his hand and forearm into the donkey's mouth, when the poor beast had a spasm and died—of lockjaw! An iron bar had to be used to release the unhappy amateur practitioner.

Many of the time-honoured remedies needed a good dollop of faith in their application but there has been great advance during my life-time in the scientific treatment of animal diseases, one of the most remarkable achievements being the cure of milk fever. I can remember when the veterinary surgeons simply did not know what to do for it and, unfortunately for the farmer, it was always the pick of the herd that developed it as they came to their prime with their third or fourth calf; poor milkers were never affected. I was taken to Radford Hall as a small boy, where they had a fine dairy herd of seventy shorthorns which supplied milk to Leamington. A lovely red cow was lying flat in a loose-box, very distressed, and half a dozen people were standing round watching her die, unable to do anything for her. Some farmers used to find that pumping up the udder with a bicycle pump gave relief on occasion, but the present method is to inject calcium into the jugular vein. The result is immediate; one moment the cow is prostrate and unable to get to her feet, the next she is up and grazing!

I thought I was being introduced to a new bovine disease one day when I asked after Hitchman's cow, which had been looking distinctly under the weather and was being treated by the vet. Hitchman, a typical old countryman, provided the village with milk from a couple of cows, timed to calve to keep up a continual supply. It had been a dry summer and his paddock was grazed down to the bare earth, and in answer to my enquiry, 'How's the old cow this morning?' I got the astonishing reply, 'The vet says she's full o' dirt from that old field of mine and it's all 'cumulated in her Bible'!' It was the first time I had come across a religious cow, but I learnt later that a lot of old countrymen refer to part of a cow's stomach as her Bible, resembling, as it does, a number of superimposed leaves.

The modern young farmer, though he may be college-trained and able to produce more with less labour, is not the craftsman that his father and grandfather were, nor has he, I think, the same satisfaction in his job; the machine has come between him and his farm and he has not the intimate contact with stock and land which taught us of an older generation so much. A little know-how saved a lot of trouble!

The management of grassland, for instance, has completely changed in the last seventy years. When I first started farming at the beginning of the century, we took advantage of the eating habits of different stock and selective grazing was widely practised to keep a meadow in good heart. Horses are the worst grazers; they will eat part of a field bare and drop their dung in another; cattle tend to drop their dung near the hedges and unless someone goes round with a fork and throws the cow-pats away from the fence, the growth will come rank there; sheep are choosey and avoid the coarser grasses. I knew one of the Strouds, the big cattle dealers of Banbury, who had a hundred-acre field; towards the end of the season it would begin to look a bit patchy, so he would graze it as hard as he could with his own stock and then, to clear it up, give what keep was left to a horse-dealer, Spencer Holtom, who was bringing droves of hungry New Forest ponies to sell at the autumn Horse Fairs. They had to eat the rough patches, or starve, and by the time they had finished their job, one could chase a mouse across the field from one side to the other! After they had gone, the place was harrowed and shut up for the winter and in the spring it looked like a lawn. Where land was understocked, which used to be all too common, most farms having little arable and far too much grass, the practice was to put a match to the patches of roughage in the spring, but this was not as good as grazing them off in the autumn.

To-day there are few old pastures and, incidentally, almost none of those enormous and delicious field mushrooms that we once enjoyed with the rashers of bacon at breakfast. The modern method is to strip-graze cattle behind electric fences and this is normally effective in keeping the animals where you want them, as they soon learn to give wire a wide berth. That point reached, the farmer may think that he can economise on his power bill, but now and then one comes across an artful old cow which has found she is being tricked. I know of one which will walk along a fence swinging her tail from side to side and touching the wire to find if the current is on or off. If off, she was jolly soon in the crops from which she was supposed to be barred!

Then take the case of stock management. I knew a highly successful farmer, Bob Berry, who used to boast, 'I never buys ought but an entire, a bull, a boar, a tup, or a cock bird.' By this method he kept disease away, for apart from the sires, all his stock was bred on the farm and more or less immune from ailments to which stock, bred elsewhere and brought in might succumb.

When other farmers were tumbling over each other to buy store cattle, he was a seller; when other farmers were giving away their broken-mouthed ewes and replenishing their flocks with younger ones, he supplied them; and so on with all his animals. However much others might show on their grazing, his sales represented actual produce from his farms.

* * *

One of P.J.'s favourite tales was about a village boy he used to know who had such a remarkable voice that he was sent to Westminster to join the Abbey Choir, the authorities there making themselves responsible for his care and education and putting aside for him against the day when his voice would break. On one of his visits home he was asked to sing a solo at the morning service in his old church.

'What do you think of Frank's singing?' Payne asked the old sexton at the end of the service.

The old fellow was feeling a bit peeved at the fuss everyone was making of the boy. "E may be able to get them 'igh notes,' he admitted grudgingly, 'but I could sing 'is damned yead off in "'Oly, 'Oly, 'Oly"!'

CHAPTER ELEVEN

Game Birds and Wildfowl

TOM SMITH, ONE of the men with whom I often shot, owned a lot of land near Moreton-in-Marsh and several large coverts scattered about the district. His energy was phenomenal. It was said his stride was four-foot-six to the yard, and he thought nothing of walking twenty miles in a day as long as he had a gun under his arm; understandably few people cared to go with him a second time for what he called 'a walk round,' but I was young and very keen and often had some excellent sport with him.

His dogs were as remarkable as he was himself. Jock was the one I remember best and though he would not have gone far in a field trial, he was the cleverest dog I ever saw. When others failed on a runner, someone would say, 'Where's old Jock?' and Jock would be laid on and the shooting proceed; it was a hundred to one he would come up presently with the bird.

He used his brain to a remarkable degree. If a rabbit jumped up out of shot in the middle of a field and made for shelter, he never gave chase, but after a quick glance to be sure of the point to which the rabbit was heading, he would cut along under cover of the hedge and be there, waiting for the rabbit like a Rugger full-back. I have seen him catch dozens in this way. He had his reservations, however, and would never go after the same bird twice. I re-

member seeing him make a clever retrieve of a strong runner partridge, but when his master fumbled in taking it from him and the
bird got away, Jock could not be persuaded to take the slightest
interest.

Tom's wisdom in the ways of the wild was worthy of an Indian
hunter and a constant source of wonder to me. He would say as
he walked along a hedge, 'There's a cock pheasant in front; you go
ahead and I'll bring him up to you.' He usually did. It took me some
time to puzzle out how he knew there was a bird there, but the
explanation was quite simple; he tracked it down by seeing its
foot-prints in the cow-pats, and not only could he tell a cock's
foot-prints from a hen's, he could tell whether they were recent,
or not.

Though most of my shooting in the early days at Neighbrook
had perforce to be confined to such game as the Midlands provided,
I was able to accept occasional invitations to go north for the grouse
shooting and the 'Glorious Twelfth' became one of the most
important dates in my calendar.

Looking back I can recall very little about the bags we made
unless I turn up my old diaries, but my memory needs no aids to
recall the sounds and sights of the untamed moorland regions of
Galloway. I think I can still hear the curlew and the bleating of
sheep, the challenging calls of the grouse and the wild cry of a pair
of greenshanks that nested on Round Fell. There was a certain
boggy place where peat had been dug, exposing the butts of
enormous Scotch firs, part of the old Caledonian Forest, and here
the spaniels flushed a landrail. Occasionally we caught a glimpse
of wild goats and were amazed how quickly and without appear-
ance of hurry they could do a disappearing act.

After an interval of many years I went back to the area and while
grouse-shooting at a particularly remote spot not very far from
Round Fell, we came upon an elaborate memorial and I learnt
that my earthly paradise had some grim pages in its history.
Straighton, the keeper who was with us, said the monument

marked the place where Graham of Claverhouse had killed three Covenanters.

Straighton was a dour old fellow, as might be expected of one whose calling made him the enemy of half his fellows. He saw active service during the war and when he was brought into the field hospital, wounded and complaining, another wounded man, an old poacher from Gatehouse-of-Fleet, recognised his voice. 'What on earth did you bring that noisy old devil in here for?' he demanded of his bearers.

I used to feel a bit depressed as I headed south again after one of these holidays, for the industrial belt of England compared badly with the moors I had just left; but directly I reached Rugby and was in my native Warwickshire, I was all eagerness to be home, where I knew I should find everything in apple-pie order; and if I could no longer hear the hectoring 'Go back! Go back!' of the old cock grouse, the familiar chizzicking of the partridge would console me.

How I enjoyed that first walk round my farm and how surprised I always found myself at the progress everything seemed to have made, progress that would have crept on me unawares if I had been about all the time. Although I could never tell whether or not my men were pleased to see me again, I really believe they tried to show what they could do in my absence.

Grouse shooting was not the only excuse I found for taking my gun far afield; towards the end of the year I tried to spare a few days to go to the east coast for wildfowling, often to Wells-next-the-Sea where I used to stay with Sam Bone, one of the wildfowling guides. I have never forgotten his flock mattress—it was impossible to turn over on it! Even so, it was much more convenient to stay with him than at one of the inns.

Wildfowling is a sport unlike any other form of shooting and the odds are heavily weighted in favour of the goose; indeed, half the attraction lies in trying to outwit such wily birds, well able to look after themselves. There are risks involved. On two different occasions I have seen a friend stuck in the mud—not a pleasant sight; I quite thought one of them would never get out, as the tide was running very fast.

My first expedition stands out in my memory, though it was well over fifty years ago. My friend and bank manager, Arthur Sheldon, had invited me to go down to Wells with him and on a perishing November morning we found ourselves floundering in pitch darkness after Sam Bone, across the salt marshes near Stiffkey. We clambered in and out of muddy creeks half full of water until we arrived at the edge of the tide, where Sam placed Sheldon in a hide among the marram-grass. Then he pulled out a compass and a small electric torch, taking care to keep the light under his coat, a necessary precaution as regards both geese and coastguards. Having got his bearings he started to wade out into the sea and I followed.

The tide being at ebb, the water was very calm, though soon over the knees of our waders. I kept expecting Sam to step into a hole, but he plodded steadily on, apparently heading for Heligoland, till in about half a mile we came to two small banks of sand and shingle. He produced a shovel from his bag and scraped a shallow pit in which I lay down on my back, while he went on to the bank a little on my left.

With the first streak of light came a chorus of bird calls heard against the plip-plap of the receding tide; I picked out the cries of gulls, curlew and plover—a complete contrast to the inland dawn chorus, but full of music. Then, at last, we heard the geese coming in from the sea. As they got nearer I could just distinguish a long, low line heading straight for my hide, but some instinct must have warned them of danger and they sheered off just out of gunshot. The naturalist in me took over and I was so intent on watching them that I did not see a small lot that came in from a different angle right over Sam; I heard him fire twice, there was a terrific rushing noise and an awful thud and a pink-footed goose fell within a couple of yards of me, splashing me all over with wet slub!

74

That was not the first time, nor the last time that I came back from morning flight empty-handed, for however much I learned about wild fowling, the geese seemed to know a fresh trick to play me. One morning a skein came head-on into a strong wind straight for where I was waiting. I thought they were within gun-shot, but when I fired, giving too much lead, they suddenly appeared to be flying backwards! Of course they were not; they were using the wind to lift them higher, and when they had decided they were out of range, they came on again, right over me—a few flaps had lifted them about a hundred yards. I believe that if, after firing the first shot, I had realised my mistake and fired the second at the tail of a goose, I should have got it in the head.

Just once I was lucky enough to see a huge flock of migrant geese, quite two thousand strong, return to the Wash. Their wild music could be heard high up in the sky long before we sighted them, skein after skein; then as they approached a point over the edge of the Wash, the leader seemed to tumble and in a series of swerves landed out on the water. The entire company followed suit, the remarkable thing being that each bird appeared to fly to the exact point reached by the first before abandoning itself to the descent. There was a note of joy in their calls as they located their beloved Wash once more, wildfowlers call it whiffling. Rooks will do very much the same in very fine weather.

Sometimes when the urge was upon me, I went to Romney Marsh. An old fellow there, Brooky Clark, had a large-bore, single barrel, muzzle-loader; he also had a very poor opinion of modern powders and, running out of his favourite black one day, when several of us were together, he begged three twelve-bore cartridges. They were loaded with smokeless powder, but this did not prevent him cutting them open and charging his old spout with the contents of the lot. Then he stalked up to a bunch of curlew behind a breakwater and fired . . . True, he knocked five over at about a hundred yards' range, but the recoil laid him flat on his back in the mud; he was more than lucky that his old gun did not burst!

After I left Neighbrook, but long before the Humber was declared a sanctuary, two fellow sportsmen and myself were on a 'wild goose chase' in the district and made friends with the lock-keeper, Tom Henderson, one of the finest wildfowlers in the country. He invited us to go with him one afternoon, promising to show us some teal. He led us along the sea-wall, or 'watcher,' till we were opposite Whitton Island, and we crawled up through the marram-grass and peeped down on the Humber. A boat had been wrecked, or had jettisoned part of its cargo of grain in the estuary, and this was drifting ashore, and a single line of feeding teal marked the water's edge as far as we could see in either direction When we alarmed the birds, they rose with a roar like that from a football crowd when a goal is scored. We shot eight; they all fell in the Humber and Tom's retriever Ben soon brought seven of them in. The eighth was rapidly slipping away on a four-knot tide and we thought it lost, but Ben, waved on by his master, soon overhauled it.

The teal were not the only spectacular sight of that afternoon. Just as the light began to fade, an enormous flight of duck flew down the Humber towards the sea; the greater part were shelduck, but there was a sprinkling of mallard, teal and widgeon, and an occasional goosander, its whiteness picking it out from the others. They were flying with a determined air as though they were setting out on a long flight; perhaps they were off to the estuary of the Elbe where the old birds go annually to moult.

CHAPTER TWELVE

Amo, amas, I love a lass.

DR. ARNOLD

AS MY STOCK INCREASED, I found myself in need of a larger acreage for sheep and I rented a small grass farm that ran the length of my western boundary and had two large fields, Hyde Barn and Bean Furlong. Both pieces of ground had been neglected for many years, partly because no house went with them; different people had taken the farm from time to time for the summer grazing, but its proper upkeep seems to have been nobody's concern. Some of Bean Furlong was so covered with ant-hills that one could jump from one to another, each hill coated with rabbit dung, which I understand, is very rich in potash—or is it phosphates? I could have made half the rent from the sale of rabbits and their skins! Old Beale spent a whole winter levelling the ground and during one very cold spell he was surrounded by starving starlings that almost got in the way when he turned an ant-hill over, exposing the'eggs,' a delicacy for which all birds will sell their souls! I used to go to see how he was getting on and one bitterly cold day he greeted me with, 'You needn't have come this morning; I've got to work to keep warm.'

Hyde Barn sloped to the north between Galloping Lane and the Paddle Brook; there was a gravel pit in the corner nearest Paxford and it had a good spring, which, incidentally, was the head water of the stream. As its name implies, the field also had a barn. A great quantity of Early Purple Orchids grew there, the colour varying from deep purple to white. It was here that I found how to shoot a head-on, driven partridge and I soon discovered that it was a sitter and much the easiest shot of all driven birds, the impact of the bullet meeting an on-coming target. I had had lots of advice, some of it contradictory. One fellow sportsman said, 'Stand with your knees bent and straighten them as you shoot!' another said, 'Stand with knees rigid and bend them as you pull!' and a third, 'Stick your chest out and let them have it under the chin!' Each man to his liking—I had to find out the best way for myself by trial and error.

Bean Furlong was a more interesting field; it sloped south from the lane to the Neighbrook and was of very old turf, so the name must have been given a long while before I knew the place. In part of it there was an ancient and very neglected orchard, with half the trees lying on their sides, but still bearing fruit, and one year I sold the crop on the trees, plus a few at Neighbrook, for a hundred pounds; the purchaser gathered twenty-four pots of Blenheims from one tree alone.

In addition to the orchard there was a little coppice on the brook bank, called the Duck's Nest, a favourite place with birds. It had a small rookery in one corner and I once found a nest of skeleton leaves with a clutch of most attractive eggs—I speak as a one-time collector—a nightingale's! unfortunately the coppice was just too far away for us to hear the cock's song from the house. Since that time nightingales have become very rare birds round here, for which some people blame the Little Owl. Another uncommon bird, the Black-capped Willow Warbler, nested in a hole in a willow tree nearby. It was easy to identify its song, not so the strange bird sounds we heard from the coppice one year — no wonder, for they came from a peahen! She must have strayed there from some distance, as I knew of no one near who kept peafowl. She laid a clutch of eggs, some of which I put under a hen, but they were infertile.

After I had farmed these fields for a couple of years, they were put up for sale and I bought them. I had paid 26/- per acre rent and bought on that basis, 26/- capitalised at 5%. There was a heavy tithe on the ground which I paid to Queen Anne's Bounty, but I did not mind that as I had not to find so much capital at the time of purchase.

About the same period that I acquired this extra land, I heard that Middle Ditchford Farm on my eastern boundary was likely to come on the market and I asked for the first refusal. It was a handy little property of a hundred-and-twenty-two acres, lying between the Paddle Brook and Galloping Lane, plus two small fields to the south; it was well-watered, had a good cart-horse stable, and a house that, though poor, would be useful for my carter, George Hall. I knew the owner well, Mr Greenhill of Shipston-on-Stour, grocer and butcher, who was noted through the Midlands for his hams, bacon and, particularly, for his honest-to-goodness pork pies, stuffed with little cubes of meat, not the odds and ends of the slaughter-house. He had bought the farm as a venture not very long before, as he had had so many contacts with farmers in the way of business that he wanted to have a go on his own. Understandably enough, the first thing he did was to build a row of sties! He put in a manager and went off to the Shorthorn Disposal sale at Kingham Junction and bought a number of pedigree cattle, but without anyone to advise him. They were not the sort on which to found a herd and after a while he grew tired of them and of the man he had engaged to look after the farm and decided to sell out.

I had to borrow most of the purchase money from my father, but the opportunity to add usefully to Neighbrook was not to be missed and I became the proud owner of one square mile of Old England—less four acres, to be exact!

I had always got on well with Mr Greenhill and when I took possession at Michaelmas he planted one field of wheat for me as a bit of luck money. There were some fine elms on the farm, a little past their best, and I sold these to help to pay for the extra livestock I could now accommodate. I never seemed to have any money in the Bank, but, as one of the Shipston auctioneers used to say, 'Stock's as good as money.' 'Blue Greys' were fashionable then and I bought thirty Black-Polled heifers and a White Shorthorn bull, with the idea of breeding for a sure market.

It was during this period of expansion and venture that I went off one day with my gun to a rough shoot and met Charles Hitchins for the first time—but not for the last!

Charles was the son of Dr. Hitchins of Brailes and was one of a family of sixteen, most of whom lived to get married; he had a quiverful himself, one delicate son and six unmarried daughters, all very good-looking. Apparently he was prepared to run the risk of having me for a son-in-law and I was invited to Burmington Manor, some six miles away.

The Manor had a large garden with tennis and croquet lawns. Till then I had found a bit of shooting and fishing all the recreation I required, but I soon had to buy some respectable flannels and a tennis-racket. I must have caused some amusement at first, but the girls quickly knocked the pat-ball out of me and made me serve overhand. I also had to do a share of the rolling and cutting of the lawns, for old man Hitchins was a tremendous worker himself and had the knack of getting a bit of hard labour even out of the likes of me!

Looking back, that summer seems to have been a long succession of tennis parties and before it was over, Claire, the middle daughter, and I were engaged. I was a lucky man. Not only was she very athletic and played a good game—she had a double-jointed elbow —but, much more important, we had many tastes in common, for she was a born countrywoman, caught many a good trout and even did a little shooting. I bought her a William Powell twenty-bore and how her father beamed when she brought off a good shot! Add to all this that she was an excellent housekeeper, liked cooking and did it well and never had any servant problems. One would have thought that Neighbrook, so remote and isolated, was the last place where a maid would want to stay, but we only had two in all the years we lived there. The first, Mabel Kempson, more or less engaged herself; when she heard Claire was getting married she begged to come and work for her and only left us to get married herself. Her successor, Nancy Dyer from Wolford, stayed until she, too, married and even then she came one or two days a week to help us. She knew how to handle a fork as well as a broom and would lend a hand in the hayfield if we were pushed. She did not enjoy good health, but is still very much alive, in spite of a host of grandchildren!

I repeat, I was a lucky man!

The garden at Neighbrook was nothing to write home about when I first went there, in fact, some of it had got very out of hand, but being young, with no time-wasters like wireless and television to distract us, Claire and I set about it with a will. Among other things we made a big herbaceous border. I have never had such a show of flowers since; beginner's luck, perhaps, but my father-in-law was a super gardener and we simply had to show what we could do.

I also levelled a piece of ground and made a full-size tennis-court; no mean accomplishment. I took great pride in keeping it rolled and mown and I could have cried one morning when I found that visitors had left the gate open and my cows had got in. We had had several very wet days and now the whole lawn was pitted with great holes, several inches deep. I was busy filling them in with sand when a friend arrived. 'You've no need to do that,' he said. 'Lend me a strong, four-tined fork.' He went round a hole, prising it up into an 'anthill,' then ran the roll over the lot and levelled it. I followed his example and in a very short time the lawn was as good as ever and one could not see where the holes had been.

But events were on the way that would make damaged grass seem of little moment. One August night found me running and stumbling across the fields to fetch the doctor from Paxford, telephones being still a luxury, and not, as now, a necessity.

'I'm afraid we are going to find ourselves at war,' said the doctor, as he drove me back to Neighbrook.

I was not interested. I had worry enough of my own, for Claire was desperately ill.

Next day was August 4th, 1914, publicly and privately memorable, Wallace Aubrey Seymour was born and Britain declared war against Germany. The first brought a new and demanding voice into our household, the second a new and demanding call on agriculture to save the country from possible starvation if food supplies from outside should be cut off. The old order had changed overnight.

*   *   *

Window-glass can become a mirror if there are trees near the house and birds flying into a looking-glass garden may break their necks. Among the casualties I have picked up have been a sparrow hawk and a greater spotted woodpecker. Bats, with their in-built radar system, are not to be deceived. At one house I have occupied there was a window over the fireplace and if the blind was not drawn when the lights were lit, moths used to flutter up and down the glass outside and on a warm evening we could watch the little pipistrels pick them off without pausing in their flight.

CHAPTER THIRTEEN

A Farmer at War

I OFFERED MYSELF for military service at the beginning of the war, but my lameness disqualified me and I was sent back to the land.

The pessimists croaked that things would never be the same again and it is certain that, as far as the farming community was concerned, the winds of change began to blow with uncommon force and we suddenly found ourselves very important people, so important indeed that we could no longer be left to our own devices. Agricultural committees, hastily organised, came into being all over the country. With more enthusiasm than practical knowledge of food production, the well-intentioned wielders of 'little authority' often rubbed the farmers the wrong way; men who had always managed their own affairs did not take kindly to dictation, especially when it ran contrary to their experience and knowledge of local conditions.

I remember an official from the Government, his name was Davies, coming to see me and telling me I must plough up more land. I protested that I had already ploughed more than my neighbours. 'Don't worry,' he said soothingly; 'it's not you we are getting at, but the Chairman of your Agricultural Committee!' That was the end of the matter as far as my own fields were concerned, but I heard the Chairman had had to come into line and do his stint of ploughing.

There was no need of a spur to make me determined to get as much as I could from my land. One of the first things I did was to buy a Ford tractor; and, as if that were not enough innovation for a while, I turned my attention to milk production. I had advertised a bunch of heifers for sale, but the man who came to look at them, a very successful dairy farmer from Sussex, persuaded me that I had much better keep the heifers he had come about, as they would be good milkers, and sell him the thirty black-polled ones that I had meant to retain. The upshot was that I abandoned my plan to breed Blue-Greys and signed a contract with a London firm to supply winter milk. Those were the days of hand-milking and my decision was much influenced by the closure 'for the duration' of the Aston Magna brickworks, which meant that I could get the additional labour I required by employing some of the men thrown out of work.

When the scheme was under way, the milk was sent off every morning from Blockley station and, to my annoyance, the station-master insisted that I waited to put the cans on the train. Waiting was not an easy role for me, nor for the restive horse between the shafts of the empty milk-float in the station-yard, and eventually I paid the man to get the loading done for me, though I am sure he was not entitled to make such an exaction.

In the old days when labour was very badly paid, especially in the case of those working on the land, the cowman and the shepherd got an extra shilling or two a week because their job involved a certain amount of Sunday work; but after Joseph Arch's championship of the agricultural worker began to take effect, a lot of farmers realised it was time they sat up and scratched their heads, if they did not want to find themselves short-handed. One of my neighbours, with a large herd of milking cows, had installed one of the early milking-machines, but with no intention of using it; it was only there as a warning to his muttering hand-milkers! That was over fifty years ago. He was a cheese-maker and fed a lot of pigs on the whey and homegrown meal.

The modern milking-parlour is a revelation to any farmer of the old school, like myself, in its efficiency and hygiene, but the drumming of the motor is a poor exchange for the musical thrum-thrum of the milk hitting the bottom of an empty pail, and if anything goes wrong with the machine, or there is a power cut, pandemonium prevails!

I recall a day of dreadful crisis at home when I was a boy. We always kept a house cow and the cowman from Shrubland Hall came in to milk her on his way to and from work, but one day he was taken ill and did not turn up. Not a soul in the neighbourhood had the foggiest notion of what to do. Finally my father decided to try his hand and I remember how irritated he was when my brothers and I came to watch the performance. I can see him now as he stooped gingerly over the bucket, and when the quiet old cow moved a foot he nearly jumped out of his skin! The cow was a good one, giving up to four gallons a day, but my father's efforts resulted in about half a pint of dirty milk.

Besides greatly increasing my milking herd I increased my flock of sheep. My shepherd was a strange little man, who came to me like a brownie, out of nowhere; but after a while he disappeared into nowhere again, because he could not stand the wrench when it came time for the lambs he had tended to go to market, and Claire, with the help of a land girl, took over his work and proved herself a born shepherdess. Dipping and shearing I would not let her do; those were heavy tasks even for a man.

I used to take the sheep to Ebrington Washbrook before shearing, but the fleeces lost so much weight that the difference in price between washed and unwashed wool did not compensate for the bother. The brook was noted for its water-cress—above the dipping tank—and Mr Gander, our local surveyor, cycled the six miles from Shipston-on-Stour to get some, but found when he arrived home that he had a lovely bunch of brooklime instead! He was obviously no botanist and often told the tale against himself. I remember there was always a good trout in the wash-brook well.

As time went on, more and more land went under the plough, my Fordson making short work of our heavy soil. Ploughing may be a monotonous job, but it is satisfying and I do not know anything like the scent of newly-turned earth to give one an appetite and make one sleep. Once, when I had been driving plough all day —I was a farm pupil and still a growing lad—I fell asleep over the kitchen range after a hearty supper. I do not know how long I slept, but I wakened in a cold, pitch-dark room and when I tried to stand up, my chair came too—the other pupils had tied me to it! I crept up to bed and it was morning and milking-time before I could turn over.

Although the old turf grew some good crops, we were troubled with wireworms and frit-fly, the latter a pest which seemed to work from the hedges inwards and spoilt some promising winter oats on Ewe Ground. I found that beans seemed the safest thing to plant on newly-broken land and a very pleasant, fragrant crop it was too. A small portion of mine in Little Ploughed Field was thinned out by crows, and though I got up very early in the mornings to scare them with a shot or two, they were like Oliver Twist and soon back for more. A litter of fox cubs, sent by their mother to play in the middle of the field, laid about half an acre flat, but that I did not find out till it came to harvesting. It is interesting to note that in the pre-machine era, beans were sown by hand, a woman or boy going ahead with a dibber to make the holes into which the seed was dropped. It needed a good team to dib a sack of beans in a day.

A side-effect of ploughing up so much old turf was the virtual disappearance of Claire's pet aversion, the May bug, alias cockchafer, or booming dor, which spends the first period of its existence underground. When the War Agricultural Committee ordered me to plough up Little Calf Meadow, one of the Middle Ditchford fields, I was astonished at the number of grubs turned up.

Hard as we worked, we fell far short of two young farmers I knew, brothers of the name of Slatter. They happened to get two or three days leave from the Yeomanry at the same time; night clubs and the like had no attractions for them and they hurried back to their father's farm, just in time to go with him to market, where they bought two hundred sheep. They spent their leave shearing them. They lost a shilling a head on the sheep, but cleared a hundred pounds on the wool!

Rationing hit the farmer and his family less severely than it did the townsfolk, who had neither kitchen garden, nor orchard, and could not eke out the dole of meat by taking a gun and picking off a pigeon or two, or a rabbit. We were particularly lucky for we also had the Neighbrook. When I first went to the farm the mayfly were so numerous as almost to be a nuisance and one year we caught over eighty fat trout on them. Anyone who has not tasted fried trout, straight from the stream, does not know how good they can be when they curl up in the pan as though they were alive. It is curious how some things are better eaten fresh, while others, like game, need hanging for weeks, though the old idea of hanging a pheasant by the tail till the feathers gave was carrying things dangerously far. Perhaps I am prejudiced, as I don't like high game anyhow, but I knew of one sportsman who nearly died of ptomaine poisoning after eating a pheasant that had been kept too long.

A few farmers took advantage of their position as food producers to keep their table well stocked, but I do not think most of us did. I only offended once and got less than nothing out of it. On an unlucky day for me, a good bullock got stuck in the ditch that took the overflow from the spring in Bean Furlong. I sent for Will Walker, the Vet, to help us get the beast out, but it broke a leg and there was no alternative but to slaughter it. Then came the question, what were we to do with the carcase? Had we been nearer an abattoir, or a town, we should have taken it there; as it was, we looked at it and we looked at each other and then Will skinned it and cut it up into joints which we divided among my men. I had about twelve at the time and one of them said afterwards that he had had many a good sweat in his life, but never before from taking home as much beef as he could carry! It did not always work out like that. A local farmer, who had a licence to kill one pig for his household, killed two and then foolishly boasted about it in a Shipston pub. Next day a van drove up and the occupants, posing as Ministry officials, asked to see the carcases. which they promptly transferred to the van and drove off and that was the last he heard of about twenty stone of home-killed bacon!

* * *

Meat rationing was the beginning of the end of such time-honoured institutions as the Market Ordinaries, and a smart recruiting sergeant would often be in attendance at the Fairs. When things were looking their gravest and the German sub-marines were sending a lot of the food intended for this country to the bottom of the deep blue sea, and the casualty lists had reached alarming proportions, General Plummer himself came to Moreton Fair to see if there were any young men left who could be spared for the army. Horses were needed, too, as power in many branches of the Forces was still provided on four legs. Eagle-eyed officers descended on important Fairs, such as the April one at Moreton-in-Marsh where there was always a parade of entires, and com-mandeered what they wanted, often the farmer's favourite animal. They took one of mine with which I was grieved to part just as I thought I had found a mount exactly to my mind.

Red Cross sales were a frequent feature of the markets and fairs, The farmers were extraordinarily generous, giving of their best, and Frank Parsons, the auctioneer, did the selling for nix and saw that everyone present made a purchase; he even scoured his mem-ory for those who happened to be absent—I know, for I once found that I had bought a billy-goat at a sale to which I had not gone!

* * *

Neighbrook was probably one of the most peaceful spots in England during the war years and so few planes came our way, particularly at first, that we always stopped work to gaze after them in wonder; even so we were not allowed to forget the country was at war. One daily reminder was provided by the Great Western Railway. Looking down from the house to the brook and then beyond across several fields, we could see where the line approached Blockley station and every morning a very heavily-loaded goods train went by from the Edge Hill quarries, carrying iron-stone from which metal was extracted for munitions.

But remote as we might be, we had our moments of alarm and excitement. There was the day I quite thought a plane was going to take the chimney-pots off the house; it only missed them by inches! I learnt afterwards from the pilot, an American from the U.S. base at Salisbury, that he was lost and had run out of petrol, but as he approached the house a spot of fuel must have run forward and started the engine again. Instead of crashing, he made a good landing on Tump o' Trees Hill and when I got to him, his first question was, 'Where the Hell am I?' I gave him a bite and drove him to Blockley station and a few days later an army lorry arrived, dismantled the plane, loaded the sections and drove off: not the sort of thing one could do with its modern counterpart.

Our most spectacular 'show' happened, I had almost said 'as usual,' on a Sunday. It was one of those perfect frosty winter mornings that we get with an anticyclone, very still and quiet, when the faint drone of several planes came to us out of the clear sky. It was a little while before we spotted three specks at about ten thousand feet, the limit of visibility, and as we strained our eyes and necks, there was a puff of white smoke and one of the planes began to fall vertically. We thought it was going to crash on Aston Magna brickyard, but providentially it hit an air-pocket, flattened out, flew a few hundred yards at a tremendous speed and dived into the hard-frozen ground at Lower Lemington, near Moreton-in-Marsh, burying the engine. There were only two occupants. The observer was saved by his straps, which took the brunt of the impact before snapping; he turned a complete somersault and landed unhurt, on his feet, facing the plane. The pilot was less fortunate;

he went through the wind-screen, severing his nose to the cheek-bone, and was knocked unconscious. Both the men were taken to Martin's farm and after a week or two in hospital, the pilot returned to his unit and was sent out to the front, where he was shot down; I never heard what happened to his companion. We were told that they were flying so high that the petrol froze and this caused the accident.

Our third encounter with the Air Force was amusing. One morning, when the war was almost over, a small plane flew round and round above Neighbrook, and, curious as usual, I was watching it when I saw something come sailing to earth in Path Ham. As it did not explode, I went to see what it was and there lay a red object that turned out to be a rubber hot-water bottle, labelled 'Birthday Greetings from Challen Sharp to his old mother!' I knew Challen, he was one of our local lawyers in peace time, and I rode into Paxford and had the pleasure of delivering his present.

I do not know—or do I?—what my younger brother Donald would have thought of our war-time excitements at Neighbrook; he would not have found them worth recording, that is certain, for he never took the trouble to write about his own adventurous experiences. He was badly wounded at Ypres and left for dead on the field, but recovered, and being invalided out of the army and at a loose end, went into partnership with two friends. Between them they managed to buy a schooner and Donald went out to the black republic of Haiti to buy honey; it was a wild, lawless country, but had a climate very favourable for bee-keeping and there were huge apiaries up in the hills. Previously the Germans had monopolised the output, but as all their agents on the island were supposed to be interned, the natives were only too glad to find a new market and Donald bought honey by the ton. The first shipment brought in two thousand pounds and some of it found its way into the village shop at Paxford! The partners thought they were on to a good thing, but the Germans resented Britishers muscling in on their preserve and managed to scuttle the schooner when it returned for a second cargo and that was the end of that little enterprise!

*   *   *

'I'll tell you something, Master, as I 'aven't told a soul,' an old fellow said to me once. 'I was down at the bottom of the garden and I 'eard a sort of squeaking under the soft-water butt. It sounded like young rats and I got a stick ready and raised the butt a bit on one side and there was a great toad with one of them black slugs on its back and it was that old toad that was squeaking!'

CHAPTER FOURTEEN

Peace is come and wars are over
HOUSMAN

THE ELEVENTH OF THE eleventh at eleven a.m.—Armistice Day.
The Great War was over!

During four long years England had looked to the farmers to
make good deficiencies when the food supplies from overseas
were at a minimum; and if we had been hurried and harrassed by
War Agricultural Committees, we had also been able to go to them
for aid and advice in times of stress and we had had a certain market
for everything we could rear or grow.

We heaved a sigh of relief and relaxed a little; everything was
going to be all right now.

It was not long before I found that peacetime had its problems
and my sleep was spoilt for several nights by the news that Lord
Redesdale was reopening the works at Aston Magna. The men I
had employed for the greater part of the war were likely to go back
to their brick-making, and since I could not carry on as a milk-
producer in a big way without their help, it was obvious I must do
some re-organising.

I decided on a clean sweep. William Woolliams, a farmer-dealer
from Addlestrope, and his brother-in-law, Charles Colgrave, a
Banbury dealer, bought all my cattle and sheep; they took them
away in lots, as suited them, and put other stock to eat the keep till

the winter. In the spring I had a sale of horses, which were good, and of farm implements, which were not, being mostly old fashioned and what I had taken over when I bought Neighbrook; then I auctioned five hundred acres of grass keep, getting in some cases as much as £11 an acre and averaging half that sum. All I had to do from then on was to count the stock daily and keep the fences in repair. There would have been no need for me to do even that, if I had taken the chance I was given when a representative of the Eastman Meat Company rode up one day and offered me £40 an acre for the property. I refused to deal. Why should I sell Neighbrook when Claire and I were very happy there and when I was doing so well with so little effort?

I realised why, when it was too late!

*   *   *

The best customer for my grass keep was an extraordinary character named Capel, who farmed at Fletchamstead Hall near Coventry. Every now and then, when the Standard Motor Company were extending their works, they took over one or more of his fields and he had to look about for somewhere else to put his numerous and very good stock. He had a couple of fields of mine for several years and eventually rented two or three hundred acres. He was a man who liked to quench his thirst and he wasted a good deal of my time doing so. I did not begrudge him a drop of Scotch, but I did begrudge the hour or more he spent drinking it and, as he always finished off the bottle, I got a bit artful and saw to it that the one on view was about two-thirds empty.

An old farmer, who lived near Leamington many years ago, stood no nonsense from callers who would have abused his hospitality. He had a number of friends in the town who were in the habit of walking over for a drink and a chat by his fireside, and as he was an early riser and consequently liked to go to bed at a reasonable hour, he had NINE O'CLOCK BEDTIME printed in large letters on the beam over the inglenook. When nine o'clock came the visitors had to go! There was a forty-acre field in high ridge and furrow to be crossed before they reached the main road and sometimes on a foggy night, when they were a bit foggy too, they would miss the path and roam about until, attracted by the glow in their host's bedroom window, as wandering birds are attracted to a lighthouse, they finished back at the farm again.

When Capel came to Neighbrook he always brought the Apple of his Eye with him in the form of a rather fat boy, about eight years old and completley spoilt, who invariably got into mischief while his father was going round the stock—I should think he had never received a paternal reproof in his life! Capel made use of my buildings and came one day to shear several hundred sheep with the help of his brother-in-law. (Query? Why is it that so many successful men seem to have a brother-in-law who isn't?) Hill farmers wind the fleeces with the weathered part on the outside, but Midlanders prefer the reverse way, and it is surprising how white the wool looks as long as the sheep have not been penned on roots. The two men had been hard at it for some time and had a stack of immaculate fleeces to their credit, when I happened to come round the corner of the yard and caught Capel junior decorating the morning's work with the tar brush that was being used to brand each sheep as it was shorn. I shouted to him to stop and his father, looking up, went completely berserk. When Capel got excited, his voice, always high-pitched, went into the upper reaches, and on this occasion he fairly screamed as he seized a big stick and laid about his darling to some purpose. Shearing had to stop in order to clip the smears of tar off the wool.

Pre-war there were often several men on a farm who could shear, but nowadays two or three young fellows go from farm to farm with a machine. They take great pride in their work and earn a lot of money. I use the word 'earn' advisedly, because they certainly deserve all they get; shearing is a back-aching job, whether one is dealing with the heavy Downlands, which are done on the ground, or the smaller breeds, which many sheep farmers used to prefer to do on a small table with two holes for the shearer's legs.

Mention of Master Capel reminds me that so far I have said nothing of my own Junior. It is the bad boy who hits the headlines and young Wallace Aubrey Seymour was a good little chap and rarely gave trouble, though not always ready to co-operate with his parents in nursery routine. I remember certain summer afternoons, when he had decided against taking his customary sleep, when I combined the jobs of nursemaid and gardener, pushing the lawn-mower with one hand and dragging his pram after me with the other, while singing, 'Go to sleep, my little piccaninny,' or, less appropriately, 'The Campbells are coming'—my repertoire was limited.

His most notable escapade, at two minus, might have resulted in far more damage than Master Capel achieved with the tar brush, for he nearly set the house on fire. His mother and I were dressing to go to a party and Claire had laid out all her best things on a fireguard in the room where he was playing. She had only left him a minute or two when he managed to set fire to a celluloid comb, which he flung away in alarm, setting up a yell that sent me hurrying to see what had happened. I found the room full of smoke and Claire's things and the carpet well alight!

There was a four-gallon bucket kept in the wash-house for just such an emergency and I soon had it upstairs and emptied onto the blaze and this made it possible for me to collect some of the burning clothes and fling them through the window into the garden. Another bucketful of water poured over the carpet, a heavy-piled Axminster that my father had had in his dining-room, damped it down enough for me to roll it up and send it through the window after the other things, and that was the end of our one and only fire. The Insurance Company, the Eagle Star, paid up for the damage.

The isolation of Neighbrook made it almost inevitable that Wallace should spend his schooldays away from home, besides which he was an only child—and at that time only nephew among five aunts—and was in grave danger of being spoilt. As a small boy he went to a boarding school at Shipston, kept by Miss Ryder; the adjective 'small' refers only to his age, it could never be applied to him physically and when he was fully grown he could give me two inches—and I am six-foot-four. It is curious what odds and ends one's memory chooses to store and thought of the school always brings to mind Wallace's information that Miss Ryder had a boiled egg for breakfast on Sundays and, strictly fair, gave one half of the top to her favourite pupil and the other half to the runner-up!

I suppose it was the fact of having a young hopeful of my own to start in the way he should go that made me consent to become a school manager for Aston Magna, my first taste of public office. It was a thankless job and I soon resigned. Whatever we proposed was vetoed by a higher authority at County headquarters, and when we thought we were fixed with a new teacher, the parson married her!

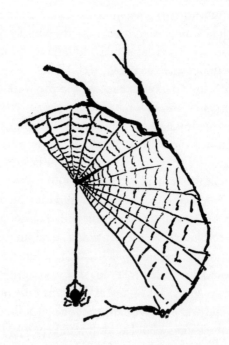

CHAPTER FIFTEEN

Of Horses Trains and Trams

NOT LONG AFTER the ending of hostilities, a neighbour rode up to my place on a fine grey which he said he had bought for fifteen guineas at the first of a series of sales of army horses at Cheltenham —he sold it almost at once for five times that sum! I thought it high time to chance my arm and next sale day I went with him to Cheltenham, travelling by train from Kingham. Prices ran higher than on the previous occasion, all but the same my neighbour bought several horses and I a bay mare that showed a lot of breeding. We took them on the railway as far as Stow-on-the-Wold and then led them from the station up the mile-long hill to the Unicorn, not an easy job as they were very fresh, having been corned up for the sale and not properly exercised; to add to our difficulties, it was a very dark night and not far from freezing.

I put my mare in a warm box at the inn while I had a bite of supper and borrowed a bridle and a damp, old saddle so that I could ride her home; but, obviously, she thought she had been stabled for the night and, when I brought her out into the cold again I had to get someone to hold her before I could mount. I was obliged to let her go for a bit and we clattered down Stow Hill and through Moreton-in-Marsh before I could check her. Nearing home, I had to turn off on that road with the nine gates; the first was so awkward I had to dismount to open it, and the mare, having got rid of me, never let me get up again and made me lead her the rest of the way. I had not ridden for months and was I stiff next morning!

The experience reminded me of the night I nearly broke my neck in my courting days, returning home after a visit to Claire. I was on a big, weight-carrying hunter that Bert Spencer had asked me to ride for a bit, a fine horse, but rather rough and inclined to rear if he did not want to go in a particular direction. Coming to a long field where the road rises considerably, I used to pull out on to the grass and let him gallop to take some of the steam out of him. I was half asleep, but I wakened with a jerk when he careered, one after the other, into three heaps of stones which had been dumped for repair work during my absence; it was lucky for me that they were spaced a few yards apart and we were going uphill! Being a very powerful horse, he did not come down at the first pile, but blundered on to the second and then to the third before he could pull up.

To my great regret, the stretch of line I used the day I went to Cheltenham has gone the way of many more that once linked the villages and small towns of the Cotswolds. It crossed some of the bleakest and highest parts of the hills, passing villages with names as lovely as themselves, Stow-on-the-Wold, Bourton-on-the-Water, Salperton and Andoversford, and one got a very good impression of what the area must have been like in the days when wool was Wool and the affluent Merchants of the Staple built those fine, stone houses, with mullioned windows, many gables and stone-tiled roofs, that are still one of the glories of the region.

Cotswold stone is of excellent quality, the warm colour varying from quarry to quarry, but always beautiful, especially when mellowed by time. The roofing tiles usually came from Stonesfield, except those for the ridge, which were from Taynton, both villages in the Oxford direction. I have been told that a bell used to be rung at intervals during the night at one quarry and the workers had to get up and pour water over the quarried stone to make it split more easily.

Seven shapes and sizes of tiles go to the making of a house roof. Those in the lowest row, the first to be laid, are called Cussens; they are two feet wide and overhang the top of the wall so that rain falls clear of the building. Above them come Long-16s—actually they measure twenty-three inches. These are followed in turn by rows

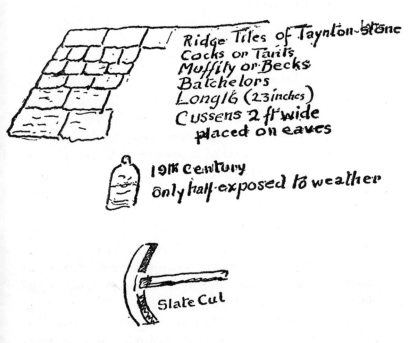

Ridge Tiles of Taynton-stone
Cocks or Tants
Muffity or Becks
Batchelors
Long16 (23 inches)
Cussens 2 ft wide
placed on eaves

19th century
only half exposed to weather

Slate Cut

of Bachelors, then of Muffity, or Becks, and lastly, immediately below the ridge, of Cocks, or Tants. Each succeeding size of tile is a little smaller than the size laid below it, and each row overlaps the previous one by half its length.

Not only the old Cotswold houses, but barns and farm buildings used to be built and roofed with stone. The farms are big and run to many acres, each containing miles of stone walls, and a handy man, who understood the art of building them, was generally among the labout force; one could always tell a well-managed estate by its walls.

There was another railway, long since closed, that I used occasionally when at Neighbrook, walking across the fields and boarding the train at Golden Cross, Stretton-on-Fosse. The time-table was elastic. I remember a long wait while the engine-driver and the guard refreshed themselves and collected various baskets of eggs, butter and other produce.

The line connected Moreton-in-Marsh, Ilmington and Shipston-on-Stour with Stratford-upon-Avon. The original section was built in 1826 and was a horse railway, afterwards dubbed tramway; it was converted to steam in 1889. Its course is still clear in many places where it runs side by side with the main road and the Tram Inn at Stratford marks its erstwhile terminus; it was only used during the hours of daylight and carried more coal than anything else. In 1864 a magazine called 'London Society' contained an article by a visitor who had made the trip from Moreton to Stratford some years previously and it gives an amusing picture of the conditions of travel before 'modernisation.' I quote:

The journey was performed outside an ordinary railway carriage which had been adapted to the necessities of horse traction. Attached to the carriage in the front was a platform on which the sagacious horse (the only locomotive used on the Stratford to Moreton railway) mounted when it had drawn our carriage to the top of the incline, thus escaping being tripped up as we descended at a rattling good speed. The Inspectors of the Board of Trade not having found this tramway, the occurrence, or non-occurrence of accidents was left to Providence. When we came to the foot of an incline, the guard applied the brake as tightly as he could; we all, to the best of our individual capacities, held on to our seats, and if we had taken firm hold, we thus managed to avoid being pitched off head foremost. When the carriage came to a stand, the horse dismounted, and drew us along as before ... At what pace we went, or whether that would most appropriately be calculated in miles to the hour, or hours to the mile, we hardly know. It was very pleasant and seemed to last so long. We are of the opinion that, except at the breakneck inclines, no great dispatch was either sought or obtained, and it would generally have been quite safe to get down and walk a little.

Some people have scoffed at the idea of the horse taking a ride, but it was common practice on mineral tramways, where there was a special truck for the animals' accommodation when going down-hill.

CHAPTER SIXTEEN

Of Dogs and Guns

CHANCING ONE LATE September day to meet an old farmer friend who used to be a keen sportsman, I said, 'You'll be getting your gun ready any time now, I suppose.'

To my surprise he shook his head. 'Too expensive! I like value for money. I've got tired of paying a hundred pounds, or more, for a share in a syndicate and only getting half a dozen days' sport with a sixty or seventy mile car journey thrown in each time. I can get all the shooting I want on my own doorstep.' He pointed to his dog, a fine black Labrador, which looked as if it understood what we were talking about. 'One day last week that old fellow tapped me on the leg with his paw, looked in my face, wagged his tail, looked at my gun standing in the corner of the room and clearly invited me to "Come on!" I said, "Not to-day, old chap!" and he wandered off, only to come back and repeat the performance. He was so insistent that I picked up the gun and followed him. He led me just across the road, put up an old cock pheasant from some brambles and I got it; then he led me down a thick hedge, put up five more birds and I got every one. That's what I call sport.'

He had a point there. On days when I went by myself round my own boundaries, I always seemed to shoot much better than when

I was with other guns, having to wait while someone else took a shot, or letting my attention be drawn away by someone else's jealous dog. Of course on my solitary rambles I rarely bothered with chance birds and many a hare was left for another day because I kept in mind that I had to be my own carrier; yet sometimes, when I brought off a gallery shot, I should find myself wishing that old So-and-So had been there to see!

For four long years I had had little opportunity for recreation and now that I had leisure, I made up for lost time and shot alone, or with others, perhaps five days a week, generally beginning and ending the outing with a cycle ride. One evening I noticed people looking at me with amusement as I made my way home, but could not understand why—I had camouflaged my hat with bracken and forgotten to remove it!

Cycling is an inexpensive means of transport and no doubt helps to keep down one's weight, but with a gun slung on one's back and a brace of pheasants and a hare swinging from the handle-bars, the return journey can be heavy going. During the war I had learnt the advantages of mechanising farm work and, the war over, it was not long before I mechanised my play and bought a car. It had many advantages: I could carry home 'the spoils of the chase' without consideration of weight, I could give, instead of accepting lifts; with petrol at one-and-six a gallon I could say with a famous removal firm, 'Distance no object,' and, perhaps most important of all, I could take my dog.

I have had almost as great a variety of dogs in my time as my father had of horses. Sweep was one of my earliest purchases. I bought her through an advertisement, without first seeing her, and when I fetched her from the railway station I thought I had wasted my two guineas, for she was undersized, pot-bellied and smothered in vermin. However, I soon got her right and she grew into the most symmetrical little bitch I ever saw. She was a cocker spaniel, from a famous working strain, and though a little impetu-ous to begin with, she needed no breaking at all and would retrieve anything smaller than a cock pheasant at a gallop. She had a clever way of balancing a rabbit and even tried to carry hares. If two of us were walking a fence for rabbits, she was so quick on them that they generally bolted within shot—and on my side. She knew at once if one was hit and often, when I thought I had missed, she would follow and return with it, but she would not go a yard after an unwounded one. During her twelve years of life she must have retrieved thousands of head of game.

I had good reason to remember one day's sport with her. There were about six inches of snow on the ground and the roads were not fit for the car, so I set out on foot with her and my gun, one pocket full of sandwiches and another of cartridges, and we went five miles across country to a farm where there were lots of rabbits. Most of them were underground, but Sweep worked the fences and I got fifteen. By that time snow was falling again and it was nearly dark and I was glad to leave my 'bag' in charge of a labourer and turn for home. Then I heard a whine behind me, and looking round, saw Sweep sitting in the road, unable to go any further! She was quite stiff and I had to carry her the whole of the five miles back to base. Fortunately I had a large hare-pocket in my coat and I put her hind quarters into it and kept one arm round her chest; by the time we got in, she felt as heavy as a Great Dane, and as for my twelve bore, it might have been a punt-gun!

Poor Sweep was stone blind for the last two years of her life, but if I was anywhere about, she could always find me.

*   *   *

It was usual on some of the large estates, towards the end of the season, to invite one or two of the tenants to join any party shooting over their fields and, in general, I have found farmers good sportsmen. Quite the neatest bit of shooting I have ever witnessed was by an Oxfordshire farmer called Parsons and his three sons. A covey of eight partridges was driven over a high hedge towards the gun on my right, who clean missed, but turned them down the line over the Parson family. What followed reminded me of the rhyme about the ten little nigger boys, for each killed a brace, Parsons himself accounting for the first and the youngest son, who had just been promoted to driven birds, the last. It seemed a bit of a slaughter, but a fine exhibition of family shooting, nevertheless.

Of rotten shots I have known many. There were two old fellows who had shot together for years and were the greatest of friends. One had never been known to hit anything moving—unless somebody else happened to fire at the same time—but he never lost hope. One day when he pulled at a pheasant, the cartridge misfired; he was much upset and showed it to his companion and asked in all seriousness, 'What should I do about this? Do you think I ought to write to Ely's and tell them? I'd have shot that bird!'

I remember standing between two notoriously poor performers at a partridge drive when a covey came obliquely down the line. I killed a right and left, the birds dropping in front of my neighbours. To my surprise they each picked up the nearest with a nonchalant air, leaving me nothing! True, they had let their guns off, but only into space; Number One had clean missed before I shot, and so had Number Two. I did not complain audibly, but I thought a lot, especially as it was the second time Number One had served me so.

At another drive a covey flew into some telegraph wires. A brace fell stunned in front of a little doctor, who usually shot very well, but had missed badly the moment before. Without the least hesitation—was he afraid they would recover before he got to them?—he pounced on them and, when the drive was over, walked along, swinging them in his hand ostentatiously as if he had got his usual right and left! Vanity of vanities, all is vanity!

I cannot claim immunity from the desire to make a proper impression on my fellow sportsmen; one of my nightmares used to be to find myself in a good stand with high birds streaming over me and my gun-barrels turned into flexible tubes, so that when I ought to be shooting, I am impotently fumbling away and was always just too late! Dreams apart, I generally find that if I miss a sitter it is a matter of sheer carelessness—but not quite always. I was walking up partridges with two other guns in a piece of roots one very thirsty day in September and as we approached a place where squitch had been burnt, a large covey, that had been dusting in the ashes, rose with a flurry. There was a breeze blowing and I was directly down wind and, just as I was about to fire, some of the dust the birds shed went into my eyes. I blinked and missed. The gun on my right, in front of whom the covey had risen, also missed with both barrels.

'What were *you* doing, Seymour?' he called.

I told him about the dust in my eyes, but if I expected sympathy, I did not get it—he laughed at me and all the comfort I got was, 'That's a new one!'

The rotten shot does no harm to bird or man, but the careless shot is a menace and it is a wonder that accidents are so rare. I have seen guns go off unexpectedly three times. All the culprits behaved in the same way: on hearing the report they instantly dropped their guns, then they cast a hasty glance round to see if they had been observed and, gingerly picking up their property, tried to look as if nothing out of the ordinary had happened.

I had three pepperings in one season and still have some of the shot in my face; I also received three holes in the crown of my hat, a salutary warning not to move out of one's place in the line. According to one of my brother Wallace's stories, being peppered may have its compensations. He took a Government post in Ceylon in a district noted for its snipe shooting, an amenity to his taste. Out with his gun one day near the irrigation tank, he shot at a low bird and plastered a native who was crouching out of sight. The man jumped up yelling blue murder, his naked chest covered with little tell-tale streams of blood. Wallace was so horrified at what he had done that he gave his victim all the money he had on him and packed him off to hospital to have the pellets extracted, but when he got down there, the fellow absolutely refused to have them removed and afterwards swanked about the bazaars, displaying his chest to all his friends with the greatest of pride!

One has always to reckon with chance. I knew a man who was blinded in one eye by a shot that ricochetted from a telegraph wire; while a friend of mine, aiming at a pheasant among some branches—there was a hard frost at the time—was struck on the cheek by a pellet that came back. The oddest accident I ever had was on a partridge drive in the Cotswolds when I was lined up with others behind a stone wall. There were telephone wires above us and, swinging at a high bird, I heard a twang as I fired and one of the wires came down and coiled all round the next gun!

And yet, while careful sportsmen can come to grief through sheer bad luck, others seem able to take appalling risks with impunity. My old friend, P. J., who knew all there was to know about firearms, had a favourite tale of a farmer he met carrying a ramshackle old gun. P. J. spotted a small hole in the left barrel and felt impelled to draw attention to it. 'Oh, that's all right,' was the cheerful reply, 'I allus holds me thumb over it!'

I had the strange experience once of seeing a bird drop before it was shot, when a field of roots was being driven downhill over a high hedge. A single partridge came first and, just as I was about to fire, it collapsed, dead! When I picked it up and examined it I found it was an elderly cock; it had probably run the gauntlet a good many times, but a sudden acceleration on seeing the guns had clearly proved too much for the old heart.

*   *   *

My doctor's description of one of his over-stout patients: 'She's just like an overflow of lava!'

CHAPTER SEVENTEEN

Of Predators

LOOKING BACK, I think one of the most striking changes I have witnessed has been in the use of the roads. About the turn of the century, a friend of mine was shooting with an elderly and somewhat eccentric country squire, who detested all traffic. They came to a place where they had to cross a road and the old fellow cautiously approached a gate and peeped over. A butcher's boy rode by, followed by a farmer in his gig, then came a carrier's cart. 'This road is nothing but a bloody kaleidoscope!' exclaimed the old squire testily. and insisted on waiting till there was a clear course before he would cross over. What he would have thought of modern traffic?

It must have been about the time my father was looking for a suitable farm to buy for me, that he asked a man working at the bottom of Long Compton Hill how far it was to Chipping Norton. 'Four miles, but it's a good' un,' was the ominous reply. As he laboriously pushed his cycle uphill, my father had to agree that the description was correct.

But as cars began to invade the roads in greater and greater numbers, hills and distances became of little account and places that had seemed far out of reach were now only two or three hours' journey away. When I acquired a car of my own, I was thinking primarily of its convenience, if I wanted to shoot away from home, but we soon found it had many other uses and it had considerable influence when Claire and I had to decide on a Prep. school for Wallace. Our final choice was one at Weston-super-Mare, which was within easy range if we wanted to run over for an odd week-end with him, or in case of emergency.

The emergency came quickly, for he had not been there a fort-night before he slipped on the tarmac going to the playing-field and broke his leg. The first time I ever spoke on the telephone was to the school after we received news of the accident. Claire and I hurried off immediately in the car and found the bones had been set and he was fairly comfortable, but he suffered a great deal in the following days because of the way the leg was laid on the bed, with all the weight on his heel, stopping the circulation; a callous developed which took months to heal. The people at the school were very kind and did all they could, except find means of relieving the pain; but as soon as we got him home, we brought a little elementary common sense to bear and supported the in-jured leg on pillows and it was not long before he was hobbling round.

It was on one of our periodic visits to Weston-super-Mare while Wallace was at school there that I made my first acquaintance with shelduck. As Claire and I walked along the front towards Breen Down on an April evening, we heard their strange, laughing call and soon spotted them, far out on the mud, a strange mirage making them look as though they were walking on air. The barred plumage was as conspicuous as the black and white of the magpie, but in a bad light shelduck can easily be mistaken for geese on account of their flight. I can imagine the wildfowler's disgust when he retrieves the inedible!

Breen Down was a 'must' for me whenever we went down to see Wallace. I particularly remember one morning when I took the ferry across to the Down and climbed to the top on the chance of seeing a peregrine, as I had been told a pair had their eerie up there.

I was unlucky. The peregrine had risen earlier than I and was probably sleeping off the effects of a good breakfast, for I came across the remains of a freshly killed shelduck with the breast eaten away; it must have been flying over the top of the Down when it was struck, as there was a trail of feathers, like a paper-chase, leading to where it fell. Not far off I found four young ravens, fully fledged but not yet on the wing; and I also saw rock-pipits and white rock-roses; the latter, I believe do not grow wild anywhere else in Great Britain. I could not help thinking what a lot of interest those people miss who never leave the beaten track, not to say the tarmacadamed paths.

I have another spring memory of shelduck, this time on the estuary of the Nith where it enters the Solway Firth. The whole of the very green merse between Glencaple and Criffell was dotted every three-hundred yards or so by a pair of them. They seemed to have marked out their territory as robins do, but I expect their burrows were on the hillside above. It was one of the prettiest sights I ever saw, though a flight of about four hundred barnacle geese came near to rivalling it as they rose off the Solway, not flying in V formation as grey geese do, but in a close bunch, all giving tongue like a pack of beagles; they did not attempt to fly round Criffell, in spite of its eighteen-hundred-odd feet, but went clean over the top.

I did not need to go to Breen Down to get a sight of a peregrine, as they often visited Neighbrook, though never nesting. My man was feeding a hundred hens under a Dutch barn one day when a peregrine flew through, scattering them in all directions; and from my bedroom window I saw a peregrine take a moorhen. A couple of carrion crows, who did not seem to know what they were tack-ling, tried to take it from her, but they soon changed their minds when she turned threateningly on them, and they went off in a hurry. There is nothing gentle about a peregrine; one alighted on an elm near me as I was driving over Joshua's Meadow and I heard the clash of its talons as it settled on a branch.

I was walking across Barn Ground in a very thick mist when there was a sudden noise overhead, which I have heard described as the tearing of calico, and a wood pigeon came through the blanket of fog, missing me by a few yards, followed by a peregrine. It was fairly clear near the ground and the pigeon made for me deliberately, but the pursuer disappeared again into the murk. I have heard that eagles and falcons can see perfectly well in fog and I think this must be so; how else would the falcon have been able to keep up the chase?

Much the same thing happened during a spell of wintry weather when I was on Tump o' Trees Hill. I saw a kestrel catch a starling' but almost at the moment she did so, she noticed me and let it go again; the intelligent small bird flew straight for me, settled on a thorn bush close by and immediately started to preen its feathers! I suppose I should have been sorry for the kestrel, for though hawks will attack most things of reasonable size, they have to be more than ordinarily hungry before they will take a starling; I understand the flesh is bitter. Almost at the same spot my presence again cost a hunter his dinner; what must have been particularly annoying was that the meal was already dressed—or should I say undressed? I was walking a few yards from a tall, thick hedge when a sparrow-hawk dashed over the top, saw me, made a quick turn and was back over the hedge again. As he swerved, something almost hit me. I searched about in the grass and presently found a yellowhammer, plucked bare, or nearly so, for I was able to identify it only by its heavy, bunting beak and a few small yellow feathers round th eye which had escaped the hawk's attention.

The sparrow-hawk is the only hawk I shoot; the others are either too rare and interesting, or largely harmless, though none is entirely guiltless of attacking game. I once saw a kestrel hovering over what I thought must be a mole, or a mouse, and waited to see whether she made a catch or not, for they have a good many disappointments. She came down from about a hundred feet to, say, twenty, preparatory to making her final drop, when a cock partridge exploded—the only adequate word—out of the grass and flew up crowing threateningly! The attack drove the hawk higher, but she returned again and again, only to be repelled in the same manner, till I thought it time to intervene. When I went to look at the place that had been so gallantly defended, I saw a hen partridge with some newly-hatched chicks.

Though normally very suspicious of human intentions, most wild creatures have little fear of cars—a sparrowhawk actually snatched a goldfinch off the bonnet of mine; and a man ploughing, whether plodding after a horse, or seated on a tractor, ceases to be an object of distrust as he plays the part of a beneficient providence, I remember a kestrel hovering a few feet above the ground when I was breaking up some old pasture, ready to catch the voles as I turned them up. I was properly grateful for its help.

For most of the small creatures that fall victim to a bird of prey, the end is mercifully swift, but very occasionally there is an unexpected hitch and the hunted turns on the hunter. I actually saw this happen. A kestrel flew up suddenly from a patch of rough grass, rising to a good height, but it was obviously in difficulties. Then I saw a weasel fall from it. One might have thought the bird would have been content to let well alone, but she stooped and caught it again before it reached the ground. This time she, managed to get a safe grip and flew quietly away. A friend of mine, George Scott, told me he had witnessed a similar occurrence, but with a difference; the bird flew some distance with the weasel, then suddenly dropped to the ground, fluttering wildly. When Scott reached it, it was almost dead. There was no sign of the weasel- it must have managed to slew itself round in mid-air and it had ripped its captor's throat open!

A member of the hawk family rarely seen in the Midlands and, indeed, infrequent anywhere in the British Isles, is the hobby. I have only identified it four times. The first one I ever saw outside a glass-case, dashed across the road in front of me near Burmington Grange and disappeared through a gap in some trees, but not before

I had had time to recognise it; the second was shot in mistake for a sparrowhawk when a friend and I were waiting for duck to flight into Moreton-in-Marsh sewage farm. It was a very handsome specimen and I posted it to my wild-fowling guide, Sam Bone of Wells-next-the-Sea, who sold it to a collector for seven-and-six—another specimen for a glass case? Let us hope it saved a living bird from the same fate. My third hobby circled round my head several times one September afternoon as I disturbed the larks whilst walking after partridges at Great Tew, and the last one I have sighted, and that only recently, flew within a few yards of me as I sat in a deck chair in my garden at Weston Mill. It was being mobbed by swallows and it was interesting to note how easily it outflew them. For a moment I had mistaken it for a cuckoo; there is something very hawklike in the latter's colouring and flight.

Another group of birds of prey, the owls, was well represented at Neighbrook, but, strangely, it was not the native species, but the Little, or Daylight owl, which forced itself on one's attention, because of its diurnal habits, its numbers and its mournful cry.

According to The Handbook, the Little Owl was a deliberate introduction into Great Britain; Charles Waterton made the first attempt with specimens from Italy in 1843, but he had trouble with the Italian Customs and only five out of twelve survived to reach England, where they soon perished. Other introductions, this time from Holland, were made in 1889 in Northamptonshire, and later in Kent. They were well established in the area when I went to Neighbrook and there were many complaints in the sporting press that they were spreading over the country to the disadvantage of many smaller birds, especially the Sussex nightingale. On an early spring evening one could hear the owls' weird mating-call all over the place; I used to stalk them and had no compunction in shooting them sitting, which to my fancy only made those that were left wail the more.

Of course the local predators resented their arrival and I have seen a kestrel attack one of the interlopers as it sat at the foot of a tree with its capture, either a mouse, or a small bird.

The only long-eared owl I saw at Neighbrook settled on the up-ended shaft of a Cambridge roller while I was sitting on the roller itself, waiting for a shot at pigeons in Coppice Ground; it looked at me for some time before flying away. A barn owl nested in a pollarded ash just over my boundary and when I rapped the tree it used to fly out over my head and more than once narrowly escaped white-washing me. As far as I knew, a tawny owl only visited us once; it flew out of a pollarded tree as I was getting over a fence; I climbed up to see what it had been doing and found a dead rabbit.

Most wild things are inquisitive. A rabbit-catcher once gave me a call he had made of two old twelve-bore cartridge-cases by punching the caps out and jamming the two ends together, and after a little practice I could give a very fair imitation of a frightened, squealing rabbit. By going from burrow to burrow I once shot twenty-six in one afternoon, all of them old bucks, be it noted. My method was to creep upwind to within gunshot of a burrow, stand stock still ready to shoot, and then use my improvised flute. Out would come the old bucks, expecting to see a stoat. They were very much on the alert and one had to be quick to get a right and left.

I often amused myself trying the call on magpies and carrion crows. If I heard a magpie chatter, I would squeal once and it was was most entertaining to note the cautious way the bird would approach, flitting knowingly from tree to tree in the expectation of finding a stoat with a rabbit and being able to make a good meal on the remains of the carcase—not always a safe practice, I imagine. From my car I once noticed something black and white bumping along the side of the road and when I had overtaken it, I surprised a stoat with a dead magpie. Reconstructing the 'crime', I think the stoat must have returned to a kill, found the magpie in possession and stalked and caught it, while it was gorging.

CHAPTER EIGHTEEN

—And Others

AS LONG AS I can remember, and that is more than eighty years,
birds have greatly attracted me and in my Prep. School days at
Leamington I often went a little out of my way to see what
Bennison, the poulterer and fishmonger, had on show. One never
knew what might be hanging up, as wild birds were unprotected
then; perhaps hundreds of skylarks on a long string, caught in nets
on the south coast, or a string of snipe from Ireland, or wheatears
on migration snared by shepherds. There might be willow grouse
and capers from Norway, black cock, grouse and ptarmigan from
the Scottish moors, or a number of mountain hares in their winter
coats—enough to make any boy late for school!

I was very small when I first began to try to draw and paint birds
and laid the foundation of a life-long hobby that has given me a
great deal of pleasure and made me observant of the wonderful
way in which nature has adapted the different species to the conditions in which they live.

South Warwickshire was rural and unspoilt in those days, and
in many areas still is; a townsman described it as 'deep country,'
and in whatever part of it I have lived there had been great opportunity for bird-watching, not only of residents, but also of passing
migrants and the odd stray, as surprised to find itself so far from its
home ground as I have been to see it.

It is noticeable how changes in farming methods have caused some birds to disappear from the County, and brought others in. The red-backed shrike, or butcher-bird, is a case in point. When I was a boy it was fairly common within a few miles of Leamington. There was one stretch of road, about a mile in length, where I could rely on seeing at least three adult cocks sitting on the telegraph lines, flirting their tails from side to side, not up and down like other small birds; now shrikes are very rare in the region, partly, I suspect, through the selfishness of a certain very rich egg-collector, who systematically took whole clutches of eggs, regardless of the law; and partly because of the change from horse transport to the internal combustion engine. Horse dung on the roads encouraged beetles, an important item in the shrike's diet; no horses, no dung; no dung, no beetles, no beetles and the butcher-bird kept further south.

I confess to having broken the law myself when I was old enough to know better. I was out riding when I saw a cock bird on the overhead wires and, knowing they had a habit of perching immediately above the nest, I soon located it high in the hedge, but not so high that I could not put my hand in it as I sat my horse and take an egg. I plead in excuse that my object was educational and intended to foster the growing interest of a young sister-in-law by adding a rare specimen to her collection, a beautiful specimen to boot, with its zone of spots on a cream surface.

It was many years before I saw another butcher-bird in my part of the County; then, on a solitary ramble—one is the ideal number for bird-watching, as it is possible to freeze in a split second—I heard the old familiar 'chack' and a moment later spotted a hen shrike sitting on the top of a high hedge. Two or three days later I saw the cock near the same place, and a very handsome fellow he was; after that I saw one or the other every time I passed. One day the cock was greatly agitated at a particular spot, and peeping over a low place in the hedge, I saw a nestling, fully fledged except for a few little tufts of down, sitting within a few feet of my nose!

It took me some time to locate their larder and, when I had done so, all I could find was a bumble-bee and a large black-beetle impaled on a thorn among some dead branches piled against a newly cut and laid hedge. Next morning I took another peep at the larder; the bee had gone and a wasp and a bluebottle were feeding side by side on the carcase of the beetle, an amicable meal-sharing that I found remarkable. I have more than once watched a wasp seize a bluebottle, sometimes on the wing, bite off the head, wings and legs and fly away with the body.

I never saw more than one of the young shrikes at a time and I do not know how many were reared; they all left in the first week of September and after they had gone I asked the tenant of the field in which they nested, and also some keen, bird-watching boys, if they had noticed them, but I seemed to be the only person who had done so.

Though we have lost the butcher-bird it is some compensation that the curlews which seem trying to extend their range. I knew of three pairs that attempted to nest within seven or eight miles of Neighbrook; it is strange that such moorland birds should try to breed in country as enclosed as South Warwickshire.

It is not unusual in very stormy weather for some sea and shore birds to come as far inland as the Midlands, particularly gulls, and it is a curious point that one never hears them call away from their home-surroundings. A man once brought me a stormy petrel that had been killed by telegraph wires near the Four Shires Stone, and these same hazards to unwary visitors brought down a cormorant, of all birds, near Shipston-on-Stour. It was found sitting in the middle of the road with a broken wing and when taken to the mill pool just outside the town on the Brailes road, it immediately began to clear the water of fish, to the entertainment of the local folk congregated on the bridge, but the anglers were not amused. Having emptied the pool, the cormorant moved up-stream, where some idle boys stoned it to death.

On one occasion an injured bittern was found in the neighbourhood, almost as far from its natural habitat as the cormorant. Bitterns are curious birds, with the eyes so placed that they can see on either side of the bill when feeding; and what excellent camouflage their plumage provides in their normal range. When they freeze in their tracks with the daggerlike bills pointed skywards, the longitudinal stripes on the breast merging with the reeds, they are almost invisible.

Most wild things are adept at making themselves unnoticeable and, sharp-eyed as I have always been, I must have been fooled innumerable times. Walking by the brook near Mitford Bridge one day, some impulse made me look back and there, lying with outstretched beak along a rotting log that was half in, half out of the water, was a mallard—watching me! In spite of its gay colouring, it blended perfectly with the mouldy wood. It was not alone; underneath the log I spotted the duck's head peeping out of the water, and as soon as they realised I had seen them, they were off!

Birds migrating long distances seem to have definite air-routes and Neighbrook was not as well placed from the observer's point of view as my present home at Weston Mill, five miles to the east; but nothing I have ever seen in England can compare to the great spring migration I witnessed long ago in Manitoba. Birds of many species were moving steadily north, some the counterparts of those I had known in England, whilst others were quite new to me. There were fresh arrivals every day. Vast flights of snow geese—Canadians call them wavies—would pass overhead, filling the sky with their unmistakeable clamour, the adults pure white except for the black primaries, the juveniles still parti-coloured; high above them, their bugle-like notes floating down to earth, went the sandhill cranes, out of sight, but not out of hearing. I was never lucky enough to see even a single specimen, but Lindsey, the schoolboy son of the farmer for whom I worked, told me what they were. All the larger birds, it seemed to me, flew very high when travelling, while many smaller species worked their way through the undergrowth; some would end their journey with us and nest on the prairie, but for the rest, it was always northwards. Then there were the snowy owls, slowly drifting through to their breeding grounds in the Arctic. I used to see one or two at dusk perched on the posts of the barbed-wire boundary fencing, their distinctive white plumage making them look like ghosts in the rising mists. They were never about during the day, but after most of the other birds had retired for the night, they would come out and wait for the Jack rabbits, an animal as big as our British hare.

Snowy owl with blue hare

It is generally assumed that birds are inclined to flock together in winter, irrespective of sex. This is true of some birds, although I have noticed in many instances that flocks are largely composed of pairs. Waiting during a partridge drive in Oxfordshire on an April-like day in December, I noticed a very large congregation of peewits in a field in front of me. Presently the whole flock rose into the air and for a time wheeled about in mass formation, then, all at once, separated into distinct pairs. There did not seem to be any groups or single birds, and I heard one or two give their breeding call. As the beaters approached, all again joined in a compact flock. I have often seen, too, how a number of jackdaws, flying together, will suddenly pair off. Wild geese are another case in point; if one is shot another out of the flock will often go to it.

Partridges seem well aware that their close season begins on February 1st and openly chase each other up and down the fields; it is amusing to see the pace at which their twinkling little feet take them, cock chasing cock, cock chasing hen and, sometimes, hen chasing cock. After two or three days of this sort of thing, the covey has broken up and the pairs begin inspecting their future nesting-sites; but if a sudden spell of winter returns, the coveys reform. In some cases several coveys will join to make a pack and then, with two eyes on the watch to each individual bird, it is impossible for one to approach them. If there is snow, they hug the hedgerows for shelter, aware that their dark plumage silhouettes them against a white background.

There is something about the bearing of a partridge that other game-birds seem to lack and I once heard an old sportsman remark, 'A pheasant is a strutting fool, but a cock partridge walks like a gentleman.' And what a model husband he is! At one time there was a covey of seven that used to come on my lawn and were always to be found somewhere around the house. When I had a shooting party I invariably contrived to save them, but one day they travelled a little further afield than usual and came back over the guns in their effort to regain what they realised was sanctuary.

Alas! they left three of their number on the ground and it quite spoilt my day; indeed, after eaves-dropping soon afterwards on a budding romance, I felt as if I should never want to shoot a partridge again. I had gone to feed some newly delivered Hungarians, which had been put in a double pen in a field of roots to allow them to settle down and get their bearings before being enlarged. As I approached, they ran into a corner and crooned and talked to each other as much as to say, 'It's all right; he won't hurt us!' and confidence in my harmlessness being established, when a covey of seven wild birds flew over, one of the Hungarians turned her attention to more important matters and called out, 'Chizzick!' Immediately one of the seven dropped into the swedes and answered her, the remaining six carrying on to the top of the field; although the immigrants had only arrived the day before, it would appear that a somewhat forward young lady had already found a local lover!

CHAPTER NINETEEN

Come wind, come weather.

BUNYAN

WHEN I WAS a lad I used to hear the old peacock at Shrubland Hall shouting his head off before rain and, if my memory can be relied on, his warning was generally justified. Before the days when one could twiddle a knob and pick a weather forecast out of the air, we had to depend on such signs to tell us when a change was coming, and in country places weather prophets still flourish and are often more to be trusted for their own small area than the official bulletin. I used to listen to the old gaffers whose rheumatic joints helped them to forecast with some accuracy, and my old rick-builder's corns were infallible—and he did not suffer in silence. I noticed that the frogs changed colour overnight, they were light yellow if it was going to rain and very much darker in fine weather; and I always imagined that the springs of water rose a bit before a switch from dry to showery. Then there was the smoke from Aston Magna brickyard that came across the brook and was a certain sign of rain; it always paid us a visit during haymaking! I love the smell of a squitch fire, or one of burning thorns, but I cannot say that I liked the smell of the smoke from the yard; there was an industrial tang to it that did not fit into the country and was one of the snags of Neighbrook that I have never forgotten. It often happened when we badly wanted rain that heavy clouds would travel along the Cotswolds until they reached the eastern boundary above Ilmington and then spill their contents beyond Meon Hill in the direction of Stratford. This was a good thing in some ways, as most of the Stratford land is on the light side and could do with a shower every week, but the land in my direction was heavy and stood a certain amount of drought.

Some of the farmers round about were notoriously unlucky with their haymaking; it seemed as if one or two of them had only to fetch out their mowing machines to upset the weather completely.

A wet spell can be disastrous at haymaking, or harvest, after the crop has been cut and before it is carted. Some farmers used to sow a little salt on their weathered hay as they stacked it; somehow that seemed to control the bacteria that caused heating and the cattle would eat the stuff, even if it was a bit mouldy. There is a saying that a fellow-feeling makes us wondrous kind, but it is poor consolation when one's own hay is spoiling, to see that one's neighbour's hay is spoiling too!

In a dry period, however much one may need rain, it is not welcome in the form of a thunder storm and as the clouds gather, most creatures, man included, show signs of nervousness and fear. Bees become vicious, cattle low and are restless, and cats and dogs creep into the house and hide in some dark corner, though I have noticed that those whose owners do not show alarm are little affected, perhaps because they have a sense of protection.

During a particularly violent storm I was sheltering in an outlying hovel when I noticed that rats and mice were also seeking shelter there, coming in from all directions. Most of them ran along underneath the manger against which I was leaning, but one old black rat gave me a look and actually pushed past my back; whether they were afraid of the deluge, or scared of the thunder and lightning, I would not know, but they were certainly in a panic.

Fear of a thunder storm is not without reason. I have seen a photograph of eleven large cattle belonging to the late A. E.

Shepard of Sutton-under-Brailes, lying dead around the trunk of an oak that had been struck by lightning; like all dead stock, they looked even larger than when alive. Personally I have been very lucky, and apart from an odd sheep, I have only lost two cows from lightning. It happened when I was farming some of Tom

Beecham's land. The poor things were found lying dead at a spot where an electric cable was taken under the Stratford-to-Oxford road near Tidmington House; evidently the lightning had struck the overhead lines and travelled down to the spot where they entered the ground. The tragedy had its amusing side. It happened within sight of the road and it was not long before the police were on the spot, all but one wearing oilskins and gumboots. They marched boldly up to the victims, or, should I say, 'were proceeding to the scene of the accident,' when the one in regulation hob-nail boots began to execute an impromptu dance; the ground was still charged with I don't know how many volts and he, unlike his luckier companions, was not insulated.

Real tragedy came very near me once. One of my men, old Wincott of Moreton Morrell, was laying a hedge when a thunder storm rumbled up. I happened to be passing by and told him to stop work and take shelter. He was very loth to break off, but as it was nearly lunch-time, he did so, laying his tools against the butt of an oak. When he came back after the storm had abated, he found the tree had been struck and his tools scattered in all directions. It is what is called 'an act of God,' though I should think His hand was better seen in Wincott's escape.

I have not forgotten how, when I was working in Manitoba, a normally quiet pair of horses bolted at a sudden clap of thunder immediately over us. They had their heads turned for home and all I could do was to sit tight and hang on to the reins. The road was level and perfectly straight, like the old Roman Fosse I have lived near for so much of my life; it had a deep ditch on either side full of water and muskquash rats, but all went well till we came to a culvert that crossed from one ditch to the other. Here the surface was raised on baulks of timber, rather bigger than railway sleepers, and when the buck-board wagon struck them I was bounced off the loosely-lodged seat into the wagon-bed. Fortunately by the time I had regained my position, the horses were leathered and glad of a breather.

It used to puzzle me how birds manage to keep dry in a down-pour. A friend and I once marked down a covey of partridges amongst a patch of pod-thistles in the middle of a large grass field, but before we could walk them up there was a rumble of thunder and we had to run to a hovel to escape a deluge. I have seldom seen such rain. It lasted for about half an hour and from our refuge in the manger of the hovel we could see the patch of thistles where the partridges had pitched. We then and there decided not to shoot them, sure they would be too wet to fly, but after the storm had passed we crossed the field to see how they had fared. We flushed them from the exact spot where we had marked them and to our surprise they rose with a flurry and did not appear the least be-draggled. My theory is that birds, when full-fledged, can keep dry in heavy rain for some time, provided they do not move about. I once got caught in a bad storm and was soon pretty well soaked, but not so my geese; they just pointed their beaks to heaven and remained perfectly still with eyes wide open, allowing the rain to run over their backs and tails.

In this Midland area, as far from the coast as it can well be, we rarely get winds that bring havoc in their wake; perhaps Stonefield tiles and thatch are less easily dislodged than slates. Even a summer gale, when the trees are in full leaf, seldom brings down more than the odd branch, though I can remember a whole row of huge elms being blown over on the far boundary of my father's field where I practised with bow and arrow as a small boy. My brothers and I had often tried, unsuccessfully, to climb them, but we were able to explore them thoroughly after a terrific wind had uprooted them and laid them on their sides; we spent hours playing in the tops, swinging about like a lot of little Tarzans. That gale must have been about 1895 and I have a vivid memory of my father getting in a panic when he feared one of the gables of the house would be blown in. He collected all the help he could and anything big and heavy and we propped the wall from inside and saved the situation.

Bad as were some of the storms I have seen, it would appear that even atmospheric disturbances are not what they were in the good old days. Sir Walter Scott in his novel 'The Antiquary,' abandons his story for several pages while he dilates on various curious documents in his own collection; in particular he refers to 'a thrice and four times rare broadside' and gives the title-page in full: 'Strange and wonderful news from Chipping Norton in the County of Oxon, of certain dreadful Apparitions which were seen in the Air on the 26th of July, 1610, at Half an Hour after Nine o'Clock at Noon and continued until Eleven, in which time were seen Appearances of several flaming Swords, strange motions of the superior Orbs; with the unusual Sparkling of the Stars, with their dreadful Continuations; with the Account of the Opening of the Heavens, and strange Appearances therein dis-closing themselves. with several other prodigious Circumstances not heard of in any Age, to the great Amazement of the Beholders and attested to by Thomas Brown, Elizabeth Greenway and Anne Gutheridge, who were Spectators of the dreadful Apparitions. . .'

CHAPTER TWENTY

The Honest Poacher

I HAD BEEN on top of the world. My grass keep had been bringing in some £2,500 a year with the minimum of trouble to myself and I had leisure to follow the country pursuits I loved, Wallace was doing well at school and Claire and I could take a greater part in social life than had been possible before. The tennis-court we had made saw much use and Claire's tennis-parties are remembered to this day. Her family's enthusiasm for the game had increased when her sister Dora married Frank Taylor of Winderton, who managed the Compton Wynyates estate for the Marquis of Northampton. He was the best volleyer I ever saw, very strong in the forearm, the result of practising for hours off a roof in his backyard. We met some very good players on his lawn.

But it was too good to last.

In the mid-nineteen-twenties, instead of getting an average of £5 an acre for my grazing, I had to be content with a mere thirty shillings and be thankful to let at all. Who could have known that the bottom would drop out of farming in such an incredibly short time? Many farmers lost all they had made in four years of war, poor Bacchus among them. He was too good a farmer for the times. He had ploughed up a lot of old pasture when he took a farm near me, drained and manured the remainder, cut and laid the hedges and altered the whole look of the place. but prices did not justify his outlay and he had to get a job as a bailiff while another go-ahead man took over the farm and reaped all the advantages of his predecessor's enterprise.

I saw the red light in time and, reluctant as I was to contemplate any change in our way of life, I had to face up to the fact that I could not afford to go on as we were and I must either re-stock and become a working farmer again or sell out before I lost any more money. Claire and I decided on the latter course, though it was a sad wrench to leave the home where we had been so happy for so long.

I put up the property for sale, but could only get about two-thirds of what I had been offered a few years before in rosier times and that only for the best half lying between Galloping Lane and the Neighbrook, which was bought by Captain Allen of the Allen shipping line. The remaining two hundred and-fifty acres I let to a good tenant, reserving the shooting rights for myself.

Claire and I took a roomy Georgian house above Burmington village where she had spent her girlhood and where her family still lived at the Manor. Several fields went with the property, well-stocked by nature with rabbits, as were the fields I still owned at Neighbrook; the obvious course was to turn a pest into a profit and become honest poacher, and with the help of a hired man I was able to deliver an average of two hundred rabbits a week throughout the winter to Mr Barnes of Shipston-on-Stour.

It was all a very long time ago. The Second World War sent me back to farming again, where new methods and new machines were trying to keep up with ever newer knowledge, solving many of the old problems that had dogged those who lived by the land—and often creating others. It was nearly thiry years before I retired again, aged seventy-eight.

I have returned to Neighbrook from time to time at the invitation of Captain Allen and it has been good to see the property looked after so well. He has made many improvements over the years, but it is still essentially the place I knew and loved, where I could see myself, a young man again, watching the lamperns in the shallows of the brook, driving a tractor for the first time in Little Ploughed Field, walking my boundaries with my gun, Sweep at my heels, finding bee-orchis in Joshua's Meadow, or laying a hedge in Barn Ground with Old Beasley. And everywhere birds.

Youth may have its visions, but old men have their dreams. How blessed is memory.

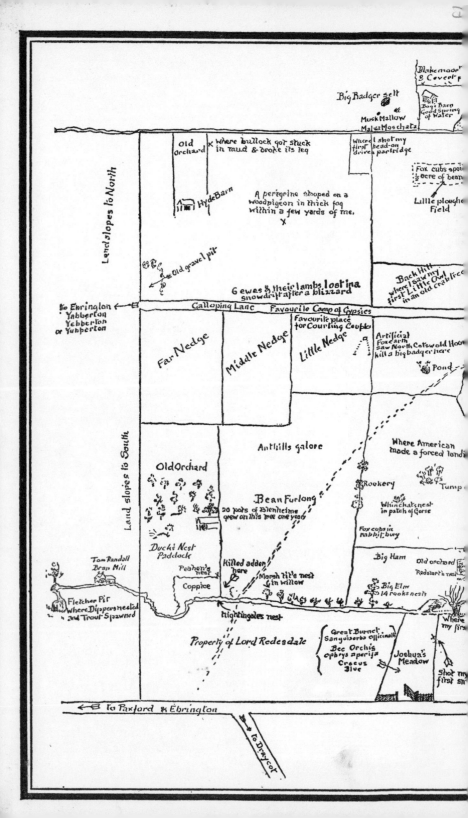